Short

Walking Tall When You're Not Tall at All

John Schwartz

Roaring Brook Press
New York

Published by Flash Point, an imprint of Roaring Brook Press
Roaring Brook Press is a division of Holtzbrinck Publishing Holdings
Limited Partnership.
175 Fifth Avenue, New York, New York 10010
www.roaringbrookpress.com

Distributed in Canada by H. B. Fenn and Company Ltd.

Cataloging-in-Publication Data is on file at the Library of Congress
ISBN 978-1-59643-323-6

Roaring Brook Press books are available for special promotions and premiums.
For details contact: Director of Special Markets, Holtzbrinck Publishers.

First Edition April 2010
Book design by Scott Myles
Printed in February 2010 in the United States of America
by RR Donnelley & Sons Company, Harrisonburg, Virginia

10 9 8 7 6 5 4 3 2 1

To Jeanne, Elizabeth, Sam, and Joseph—
who make me feel seven feet tall, even
if they have to cut me down to size
now and then.

Contents

Contents

Introduction

Everything's bigger in Texas!

That's the saying, anyway. People say that because the state is so huge—you can drive twelve hours on Interstate 10 and barely get from Orange, at the eastern end of it, to El Paso at the far western border. Texans like to do things in a big way, too, and outside the state people think of Texas as the Home of Big. Had any thick slabs of "Texas toast" lately?

So everything's bigger in Texas, except for me. I grew up there, and I've been small since I was small—that is, young. Back in Island Elementary School, I was always the littlest guy in my grade. Sometimes it bugged me. Sometimes it bugged me a *lot*.

Now I'm grown up, so to speak. I'm still little: just five feet, three inches tall. By anybody's standard, that's kid-size. And when I meet people and tell them I'm from the Lone Star State, there's always some joker who will look me up and down—mostly down—and say, "But I thought everything was bigger . . ."

Boy, does that joke get old.

I was always the kind of kid who read the newspaper, and I was always interested in science, reading about probes we had sent to other planets and the orbital adventures of astronauts. As I grew up, I read about studies that made it sound like little guys always have it tougher than taller guys: that we earn less, that we have fewer choices when it comes to mates, and that we might not even be as smart. And I paid close attention—let's face it: *really* close attention—to the developing science of hormones that scientists said could help short kids increase their height. If I had believed all of that stuff, it would have been like the singer Randy Newman put it in that old song: "Short people got no reason to live."

But as I learned more, I came to realize that reality rarely lives up to the hype.

I definitely do not have the kind of second-rate life that the studies seem to predict. I've got an exciting career as a reporter, working for a really great newspaper, the *New York Times*. I'm not rich, but I make good money, and I travel all over the world for my stories. I've dated women shorter than I am and some much taller; I'm happily married. (Okay, since you're probably wondering, she's about an inch taller than I am.) We've got three kids, and they are all taller than I. Even the youngest one, my thirteen-year-old, passed me last year. When he wants to have a good time, he stands next to me, looks down, and laughs an evil little laugh.

So I decided to write a book that could bridge the gap between what I had read and what I've lived. I've learned a lot about the science of height, and the strengths and weaknesses of the studies that try to fit our lives on a grid or chart of wealth or happiness. And I learned even more from growing up small and seeing things turn out pretty much great, and from watching the other short kids around me struggle with the same doubts that I had.

So this is a book about being below average,

and what shortness means in a world that's obsessed with being normal, or even perfect. But there are many, many ways that most of us don't qualify as "normal" or meet somebody's average. We might be too short, too big-nosed, too slow, too smart, too flat-chested, too fat, or too scrawny—there always seems to be something that sets us apart. So I'm hoping that just about anybody can get something out of reading this book. After all, did those millions of people read about Harry Potter because they have magical powers and had a tough time learning the *patronus* spell? I don't think so. But many of us, at some time or another, have felt different—and have hoped that what makes us different might actually make us special.

I was the smallest person in my family when I was a kid; I'm the smallest person in my family again.

And that's fine.

You aren't doomed to a second-rate life, either—no matter what it is that makes you different.

So let's talk for a while about being short, and all the other stuff: What if the doom-and-gloom studies about being short don't actually say that all short people are doomed to gloom? What if it's all a little more . . . *interesting* than simply saying that science proves that *short* equals *doomed*? As a science reporter, I read more closely than most people, and I ask the right questions. And I want to show you how to do it, too—to approach questions like this with a healthy skepticism, and to figure out the truth for yourself. And maybe, along the way, to help people see that being different isn't necessarily an affliction.

Now, for those who feel that being short is a huge burden, it just is. No citation of averages or arguments based on data will automatically change those feelings. I know that there were plenty of times that being the smallest guy in school felt like the biggest problem I had. But it doesn't have to be that way.

So here's the deal: If I do my job right, then by the time you finish this book you will have changed.

No, you won't be taller, unless it takes you a *really* long time to read the book. But you will be smarter. You will know a little more about biology, psychology, and human nature; and you'll be a lot better at reading scientific studies and taking them apart. You'll have a start on understanding statistics—and how they don't always say what advertisers want you to think they do. You will be better at taking apart other people's arguments. You will run faster and jump higher. Oh, wait. That's the ad for those old sneakers, PF Flyers. But the other stuff is for real.

Some of these concepts aren't easy—in fact, as you'll see, many adults don't seem to understand the things you'll learn in this book. But I refuse to talk down to you.

Stick with me.

We'll walk through it together.

The Fixers

When I was a kid, twelve cents could buy you a lot of fun. That's what a comic book cost then. I could buy eight of them for a dollar at the Piggly Wiggly store, and read the adventures of Superman, Batman, and the Green Lantern. When I was nine, my mom even bought me a Superman suit and cape, and I would actually wear them around the house. I'd jump off the couch, the cape flying behind me, and sometimes even wore the suit under my clothes just like Superman did. My dad tells me he was scared to death that I'd try climbing up on the roof to see if

I could really fly. I avoided that disaster, though. Even then, I knew it was make-believe. I would never be faster than a speeding bullet, but a boy could dream.

Reading my comic books, I lingered over the ads for "elevator shoes" and Liftee height pads that promised to add between two and four inches of height "invisibly." How did those work? The word *elevator* made it sound like there was something mechanical in there, or maybe even magical. But the shoes really just had soles that were several inches thick. Even in the ads, those monster shoes looked like they might be too heavy for my little matchstick legs to lift. I'd be taller, but I'd have to stand in one place all day.

"BE TALLER—Stand 2–6 inches TALLER in a few weeks. All ages. No gimmicks. GUARANTEED. Send 35¢. . . ."

The get-tall ads were right by the ones for big-muscle programs from Charles Atlas body-building that would—if I sent Mr. Atlas money and followed the directions in his booklet—help me follow his path from "97-pound weakling" to "the world's most perfectly developed man." Even better: Mike Marvel, who

"CAN BUILD YOU A MAGNIFICENT NEW HE-MAN-MUSCLED BODY IN JUST TEN MINUTES A DAY— with absolutely NO weights— NO bar-bells— NO EXERCISE AT ALL!"

In the years between my time as a kid and yours, a lot of things have happened. Comic books cost four dollars or more these days. And we now have spam to tell us we can get taller, or, um, bigger. But the basic idea—the idea that *there's something terribly, tragically wrong with you, and if you just give us money we will fix it*—is still the same.

The pitches have never gone away, and never will, because the marketers know that most of us believe, deep down, that in some way we don't measure up. That our bodies could be better. *Should* be better. And they think that we will pay dearly for the promise of a fix.

Sleazy salesmen have no trouble at all playing on that kind of insecurity and selling short guys fake drugs that they promise will make them taller. The U.S. government recently cracked down on a company selling something called HeightMax that was supposed to increase height by 35 percent in a year for users between the ages of twelve and twenty-five.

Let's do that math: That would mean somebody five feet tall would grow an additional 21 inches— nearly two feet. The wonderful people who pulled off this scam faked an "inventor" whose name they put in radio ads, and had testimonials from people who said their lives had been changed by the magic medicine. The ads said HeightMax would be "the answer to your prayers."

The company didn't admit that they were scamming people. Instead, they settled the government's lawsuit against them, paying nearly two million dollars in fines. But think about it: That means that even though the claims were obviously absurd, they had probably sold millions of dollars' worth of this worthless product to suckers. And that is a lesson in just how powerful the urge is to take what nature gave us and stretch it. The makers of HeightMax are not the only ones. They're just the most recent ones to get caught.

Now, don't go thinking that anybody who says he can make you taller is just full of hot air and that the only transformation he is capable of is tranforming your money into his. There are legitimate treatments out there—but some of them sound more like the stuff of horror movies than medical treatment. And while the scams tend to be harmless, aside from the money that the suckers lose, the treatments can lead to pain and disaster.

The most extreme example is a process called limb lengthening. The details are gruesome: Doctors actually saw apart the patient's leg bones and put the legs in adjustable braces that look a little like cages with knobs on them. (You *really* don't want to see the pictures.) The patient then turns the knobs a few times a day, which stretches the bone apart a tiny bit at a time. In other words, it's like a medieval torture rack, but it's applied in a hospital instead of a dungeon. The other difference is that the patients pay for their torture: about $25,000. If everything goes right, the healing bone bridges the gap bit by bit, and over six months' time in the brace the patient can get to be a few inches taller. It takes two years to recover fully.

The procedure is especially popular in China, where the government discriminates against people based on height. There are height requirements for some professions there, so being short can keep people from getting positions as diplomats, flight attendants, and more. A story in the *New York Times* said that would-be Chinese diplomats must be at least five foot seven if they are men, five foot three if they are women. The Chinese news agency says that men have to be five foot nine and women, five foot five to apply for college majors such as acting or broadcasting. What's a short person to do? Well, some folks get lengthened. And, sadly, the Chinese press is full of accounts of surgeries gone horribly wrong. There are legitimate problems, such as dwarfism or having one leg shorter than the other, that are severe enough to justify the risks of surgery, but the procedure is just way too dangerous and painful to go through just to look taller.

In 2006, China cracked down on the surgery. Mao Qun'an, a Health Ministry spokesman in China, said that it "must only be carried out for strict medical reasons."

Good luck with that one, Mao. It looks like the surgery isn't going away anytime soon. One Chinese doctor, Dr. Xia, advertises his Beijing Institute of External Fixation Technology around the world. His website says that the institute is "where science and technology meet your dreams."

Yikes.

In the United States, patients are more likely to turn to drugs when they want to grow taller. And there is a lot of work by real scientists and real drug companies to help people to grow. They aren't like the sleazy Internet guys—their treatments, depending on which study you read or which doctors you talk to, might end up buying you an extra inch or two. But there are some real problems with the way that they sell their stuff, too.

So let's talk about drugs.

No, this is not a DARE lecture. I mean medicine

to give people a height boost—human growth hormone. Like the leg surgery, it started as an attempt to fix medical problems. But, like the leg surgery, its use has spread to people who are merely short.

Human growth hormone is a chemical messenger that occurs naturally in the body and is part of the process that spurs growth and development. If a person's body doesn't produce enough of it, that person is likely to be very small, and the small person is said to have a medical condition such as dwarfism. Those people can be helped by injections of human growth hormone, which helps supply what their body doesn't.

In the early days, scientists didn't know how to manufacture the hormone, so they extracted it from the bodies of dead people. By 1985, a synthetic version had been developed and was approved for use as a medicine, mainly for those people suffering from severe problems such as dwarfism. Some doctors prescribed it for patients who didn't have those problems, though. Bodybuilders wanted it, though it hasn't been proven to actually help them. (A lot of body builders will take just about anything that they think will pump them up.) And some doctors also started prescribing the hormones for children who don't have a hormone deficiency but are just plain short. That's a big difference.

Before long, the drug companies were pushing

the government to give its blessing to what they had been doing anyway. And so, in 2003, the government did approve the use of growth hormones for short kids who weren't suffering from a medical condition—to be specific, the shortest 1.2 percent of children. For ten-year-old boys and girls, that meant anyone shorter than four foot one. The idea was that it would be used in kids likely to grow to adult heights of less than five foot three (for boys) and four foot eleven (for girls.) Did I mention that I'm five foot three? So I am officially really short. But I didn't need a government ruling to tell me that.

The phrase that was used by the drug companies and the government to describe being short was a whopper: *idiopathic short stature. Idiopathic* is one of those great words doctors and scientists use to describe something that they don't understand, something with an unknown cause. So *idiopathic short stature* means "this person is short and it's not for any of the medical conditions we know about, such as, say, growth hormone deficiency." Now, the most common reason that somebody is short is that his parents are short—we'll talk a little more about that later on. But using fancy words derived from Greek with a lot of syllables makes it all sound very medical, very disease-ish.

It's not the first time that the medical industry

has tried to sell cosmetic treatments by using a fancy medical-sounding name for the problem—they used the same trick back in the early days of breast implants.

As you might have noticed, breasts come in various sizes. Some women whose breasts are on the smaller side would like them to be bigger— and, wouldn't you know it, an industry has grown up around making money off those feelings of being too small and inadequate. The medical answer is breast implant surgery, and hundreds of thousands of women a year get the procedure done.

The companies that wanted to sell women on the idea of making their breasts bigger didn't use plain words such as *flat-chested*. Instead, they made it sound like a medical condition that needed treatment, and called it "micromastia." The companies making breast implants argued that women with flat chests suffered from a lack of confidence and would lack success in love and careers. To hear the doctors talk about it, the women were destined to have a second-class life.

Sound familiar?

And so, when the Food and Drug Administration (FDA) considered giving its blessing to using growth hormone to treat the terrible disease of shortness, one of the scientists from Eli Lilly, a hormone maker, called the condition a "growth failure problem." The scientists laid out a list of problems that short kids face that made it sound as if it would be cruel to deprive them of the solution. And the announcement from the government that the drug had been approved for merely short kids talked a lot about idiopathic short stature. It was all very medical-sounding.

Growth hormone has been a real blockbuster in the years since the approval. According to the market research company IMS Health, the growth hormone market has sales of more than a billion dollars a year.

Was the approval a good decision? Giving the drug to short kids was already legal: Doctors can prescribe any drug that's been approved for one condition to treat any other condition. But the seal of approval from the FDA was really important because it made it legal for the drug companies to *market* the drugs for the new purpose. Drug companies spend billions of dollars a year telling doctors how great their FDA-approved products are and how important it is to prescribe them. But before the FDA approval, companies weren't supposed to push doctors to prescribe growth hormone for short kids, and couldn't tell consumers—your parents—that giving you the drugs was such a wonderful idea. Whether we actually need a drug or not, we're likelier to think we need it if a doctor recommends it. Whether the drug will actually be effective or not—and many drugs do very little—we tend to believe in the promises that the companies and doctors make. Marketing also leads to bigger profits, because parents who hear about a drug are likelier to request it, even demand it, for their kids if they know it's out there. And once the doctors and parents get together, just about every kid will end up taking the treatment. After all, parents teach us to take our medicine—"It's good for you!"

FDA approval also helped to get insurance companies to pay for the treatment. That's a big deal, because hormone therapy is expensive. The cost for five years of treatment, with almost daily shots, would come to about $100,000 per kid. And if the estimates of the effectiveness given at the FDA hearings are correct, the increase in height over what the kid would have reached anyway is a whopping 1.9 inches. So we're talking about some very expensive inches: $50,000 apiece! You can buy a Lexus for $50,000.

Many kids go to all the expense and trouble for less growth than that. Stephen Hall, who wrote a great book about height, *Size Matters*, is pretty skeptical about the drugs. He told me that even if someone gets the injections and grows a few inches, "it's impossible to give a drug to someone and say they would not have grown to that height otherwise."

But even if those inches really are the result of the drugs, a short person who gets the treatment will still be pretty short, said Dr. Alan Rogol, who regularly prescribes the drugs for kids with hormone deficiencies in his work as a pediatric endocrinologist. He explained that somebody who is five foot one and takes the drug might end up gaining those two, maybe two and a half inches. The treatment is successful, but as he pointed out, the kid is still pretty short.

"Go down to the mall or the center of town," he said. "Line up all the boys [of one age] from the shortest on the left to the tallest on the right." If you marked the line into thirds, showing the shortest third, the middle, and tallest, "the boy we just described would move a very little bit within that first third."

A lot of experts say that, in other words, that kind of success doesn't mean much. Alice Dreger, a bioethicist at Northwestern University, told me, "I wish the doctors would say this: 'Your child will go from being short to being short.'"

The other problem with giving a bunch of kids powerful hormones for something other than a serious medical condition is that all drugs have side effects and risks. According to David Sandberg, a psychologist at the University of Michigan who has studied the psychology of being short, the studies so far have declared the drugs safe (aside from problems like joint and muscle pain) after a few years of use. But, he points out, that says nothing about "possible harmful effects thirty years down the road."

One of the things that Eli Lilly's supporters pushed hard during its presentation to the government for approval was that short kids have social problems and that the drugs can help fix them. The slides they presented were a little surprising to some people: Dr. Sandberg, whose research has shown that short kids actually cope pretty well with being small, was surprised to find that his work was being cited by the drug company to support the notion that the kids have big problems. Another expert who told the FDA that short kids have self-image problems and behavior problems published a study the very next year, based on the very same data that she had used for her testimony, and concluded that there actually had been "no evidence" that being short was the cause of those problems.

We'll get back to studies and how they don't always tell the whole story a little later, but for now, here's what you need to know:

***All that stuff about all the psychological
stress of being the little guy?
And the improvement the drugs
ought to bring about?***

Never mind.

Dr. Sandberg told me that he's still stunned about the decision to approve the drug for use in kids who are merely short. "If we don't have evidence that there's psychological benefit," he said, "what's it all about?" In the end, a lot of the "problems" that people associate with being short are created by the same people who say they're trying to fix them. It can be difficult to separate the real problems from the marketing hype, but figuring out how to tell one from the other can make a huge difference.

The bottom line is that being short doesn't cause mental problems. It's as simple as that. And getting a little bit taller "does not magically cure" problems, Sandberg said. "It's not like taking penicillin and curing pneumonia."

Does Size Matter?

Don't get me wrong—height is an important part of who we are, one of our most obvious outward traits. Are you smart or stupid? No one will know until you open your mouth. Rich or poor? Hard to say, until the wallets come out. Tall or short, on the other hand . . . well, it doesn't get much more obvious than that, does it?

Our culture is fixated on height—whether it's the image of a tall, dark, and handsome leading man or the towering politician, like George Washington, who stood well over six feet tall in an age when most people were shorter than we are today. Even today, the taller candidate for president usually wins.

To some extent, society seems to look up to tall people and to look down on short people, so to speak. There are lots of shops that call themselves Big & Tall, but you never see an advertisement for Short & Portly.

Why does it seem so important to many people to be tall? Some of it goes back to childhood, when we are all small and the adults—the authority figures in our lives—tower over us. We want to grow up, and that means growing. Up.

A lot of it has to do with the desire to be "normal." But who's to say what normal is? What is "short"? What is "tall," and what does "normal" mean? What is it that makes height seem so important?

The answer to those questions lies in a simple wavy line, called the normal distribution, also known as the bell curve. Whether or not you have heard either term, you've probably seen the graph of a bell curve. It's got a distinctive shape like, well, a bell. Here's one:

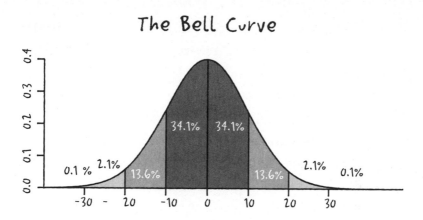

The Bell Curve

0.1 % 2.1% 13.6% 34.1% 34.1% 13.6% 2.1% 0.1%

-30 -20 -10 0 10 20 30

Well, sort of like a bell. You get the idea. This one just describes a random set of numbers. The thing that makes the bell curve such a powerful idea is that it describes random assortments of just about anything. Let's say you have a group of people and you want to measure some characteristic for each person and put it up on a chart—it could be height or weight or income, you name it. Most of the time, there will tend to be more of them in the middle than at the extremes of either end. If you're plotting income, there won't be a lot of really rich people or a lot of really poor people, so there will tend to be more of them in the middle than at either end. On the chart, the middle bunches up and the ends tail off.

Here's an example: IQ tests. There are a lot of average people and relatively few brilliant ones and relatively few who are mentally impaired. So the larger number of people in the middle of the range of

IQ scores pushes the middle of the line on the graph upward into the bell-top shape. The smaller numbers of Einsteins and, um, really-*not*-Einsteins make up the low parts on the sides. They lie outside the meaty middle of the range, and so they are called outliers.

You'll find the big middle and the little ends in all kinds of random distributions, for all kinds of traits. If you took a group of people with high IQs—say, the membership of the local Mensa club—you might have more smart people than you have in the rest of the population. After all, that's the definition of Mensa membership. But *within* the group, you would still have a clustering at the middle of the medium-smarties, with fewer less-smarties on one side of the curve and a smallish number of super-smarties on the other. (That's the thing about the bell curve. It shows only who's smart or not-so-smart *compared to the other people on the chart*. In other words, it's all relative.)

It's the same with height: Most people tend toward the average, with few very short people and few very tall ones. According to the National Center for Health Statistics, the average American male is about five feet, nine inches tall, and the average woman is a little under five feet, four inches. So a chart of men would put five feet, nine inches at the center, with most of the population clustering around that average. The smaller numbers of shorter people tail off to the left and the taller people tail off to the right.

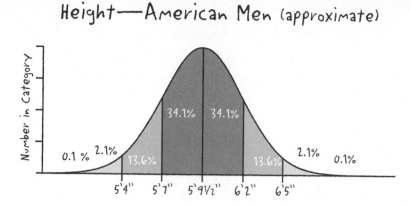

Height—American Men (approximate)

Short people and tall people stand out because they are different from the rest: They are outliers. There are relatively few of them, and a lot more of the average folks. In fact, under the normal height distribution, about two thirds of the people make up the middle chunk of the bell.

That middle chunk is referred to, by the way, as being the group that is within one "standard deviation" of the middle line. The standard deviation is a common measurement of the way that populations vary from the average. I'm not going to discuss the math behind it, which involves square roots and more figuring than I want to get into with you. But it's enough to keep in mind that 68 percent of people will fall within one standard deviation of the mean, or average. About 95 percent of the values fall within two standard deviations of the mean, and 99.7 percent lie within three standard deviations of the mean.

When the federal government approved the use of growth hormones for really short people, it worded the announcement in terms of standard deviations— those whose place on the curve is more than 2.25 standard deviations below the mean for their age and sex. That is the shortest 1.2 percent of children.

Let's take it a little further. On the next page, you'll see a chart that doctors use to show the range of height over time. (If you hate charts, just skip on to the stuff that starts right after the chart; you'll still know more about this than the next guy. But there's a lot here, if you want to take the time to look.) The chart, which is based on one published by the Centers for Disease Control, is not especially easy to read, but if you give it a long look the squiggles start to make sense. Age runs along the bottom of the chart, from ages two through twenty. The numbers running along the left and right show height, in inches and centimeters. On the lines themselves, at the right-hand side, you can also see where each line sits as a percentage, with 50 percent at the middle, and you can see the standard deviations.

You can see that the average male will end up a little under five feet, ten inches—which we already knew. Now trace that line back downhill and you see that at the age of twelve, the boy whose growth is smack-dab on the average line will be about fifty-eight inches tall, or a couple of inches shy of five feet.

A boy who is considered short, which many pediatricians say is anyone in the bottom 3 percent of the height chart, is a little more than five feet, four inches at the age of twenty; the 3-percenter at age twelve is about fifty-three inches tall, or four foot five.

Height for Age

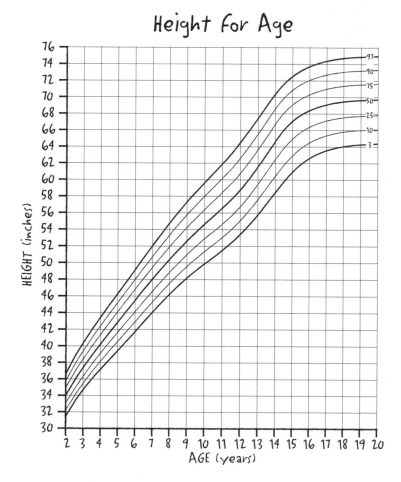

So what the fixers are trying to do is to make people think that they can move from outlier territory into the middle of the bell curve, nudging them toward normal. It's not so much about reaching a specific height but about blending in with the crowd.

Being on the tail end of the bell curve isn't simply a matter of not being a likely candidate for president, or being a target for spam artists. Billions of dollars in manufacturing decisions are based on producing products that will meet the needs of the broadest possible population of customers—and if that means leaving out some of us outliers, well, so be it.

Manufacturers try to come up with ways to measure the body—not just the average heights and sizes, but how the body moves and works as well. They want to sell things that fit the largest number of people, and they don't want to waste a lot of money making things that very few people will buy.

And this is where, finally, we get to some of the real, honest-to-goodness disadvantages that can come with being super short. In a world built around standards, outliers can have a hard time getting some of the things they want.

Probably the most ambitious and complete program out there for measuring the body is called CAESAR, which stands for Civilian American and European Surface Anthropometry Resource Project.

The program, begun in 1998, was created to take the guesswork out of designing everything from clothes to cars. The result is a set of data that can be used in the kinds of software tools that designers use, such as computer-aided design programs, when coming up with a new product. One of its biggest applications is in the military, where it's really important to make sure that pilots fit their cockpits and can reach the switches they need to be able to reach and see all of the controls. A brochure for the program carries the slogan: "Because we are not a 'one size fits all' world."

It just feels that way sometimes.

But all of those figures and measurements don't necessarily work in the favor of us outliers. In the end, it just isn't practical to design products that fit absolutely everyone. Bob Boniface, the director of advanced design for General Motors, explained to me that his company tries to make cars that are so adjustable that they will fit almost everyone—from a woman in the fifth percentile of height who stands about four foot ten to a man in the ninety-fifth percentile in height at about six foot five. That's a wide range, but it does leave some people out, he said. Very short people have to buy pedal extenders and seat boosters, and pay an auto modification shop to move the track that the adjustable seats slide on. NBA basketball players complain that they can't fit into their Hummers and Escalades without modifications, either. "Our answer," Boniface said, "is the same for them." He explained that making cars is a business. "We do our best to make everyone happy with our vehicles," he said, but "to go after that last percent" adds too much to the cost of making and selling cars to profit from the additional number of customers they would be accommodating. "You start to add a whole lot of cost for not a lot of return," he told me.

Small people also know that finding clothes that fit can be a frustrating quest. You can always take pants for a tall guy and have a tailor shorten the legs, but that leaves the pockets and proportions looking a little off. I called Consuelo Bova, who runs an online clothing store that offers clothes for smaller men, and she said that it's hard for smaller people to find clothes because of the bell curve. "The regular retail market, of course, aims to the middle—that's where the sales are." But even if you find clothes to sell to shorter guys, she said, it's hard to advertise to them. When she and her husband started their business, they ran into what she called a "marketing problem": nobody likes to be thought of as short. "It's a lot easier to market to men by saying they're big, tall, manly men than to address them as short," she told me, adding that there are "no words with nice connotations" to use with a man who is short. So instead, she said, they focus on the main complaint that smaller people have: that clothes don't fit. And so they called their company ForTheFit.com.

Of course, even if a short person finds clothes that really look great, he might still get teased. When I was younger, one of the most powerful legislators from Texas was a guy named John Tower. He didn't live up to his last name. He did not tower over people, being just five feet, five inches tall. But as a senator, and later the secretary of defense, he cut a pretty imposing figure in his tailored suits. He was very proud of them, and according to legend, he once asked a fellow senator, Fritz Hollings, if Hollings liked one of his new suits. "It's very nice," Senator Hollings said, "but does it come in men's sizes?"

Funny story! But let me just confess something: To get clothes that fit my small frame, I occasionally do my shopping in the boys' department. The first time I started looking through the kids' racks, I was pretty embarrassed about it. But now I take a kind of pride in it, as if I'm getting away with something.

And I'm likelier to find a suit that's shaped like me on those racks than on the ones for people my own age. The last couple of suits I bought actually came from secondhand clothing stores. I realized that a lot of thirteen-year-old boys are my height, and the Jewish ones get bar mitzvah suits that they grow out of almost right away. Since I now live in the New York area, which has plenty of Jewish kids, the racks are full of good stuff. The crusted cake stains come out with the first dry cleaning.

But the downsides to being an outlier go beyond the inconvenience of having your car pedals adjusted or the embarrassment of shopping in a different clothing department. The standards that manufacturers set can put short people at risk. Take air bags in cars, which save thousands of lives each year. They deploy at blink-of-an-eye speeds: five hundredths of a second. For the fat middle of the bell curve, they work well—even beautifully. But for those on either end of the bell curve of height, they can be risky. A study published in October 2008 looked at accidents involving 69,000 front-seat car passengers found that though 2.3 percent of all front-seat occupants of cars got some part of their body seriously injured when their car crashed, but that the very short and the very tall were somewhat likelier to get hurt, especially if they sat close to the airbag. Lowering the risk is pretty easy, though: The researchers, as well as the National Highway Traffic Safety Administration, recommended that very short and very tall people make sure that they sit at least ten inches away from air bags.

Some things in life, it turns out, are like an amusement park: You have to be a certain height to ride the rides. American astronauts have to be somewhat more than five and a half feet tall to go on a space walk, because the special suits for leaving the shuttle and space station come in only medium, large, and extra-large sizes. The space program hasn't built many suits, and each one costs millions of dollars. So they never made one in a small size, which means that only about two thirds of the women in the astronaut corps can fit into the space suits to take a space walk. Only eight American women have walked in space; more than one hundred fifty American men have. If I had ever been able to fulfill my childhood dream of being an astronaut (that particular dream was almost as big as the dream about being Superman, and way out ahead of the dream of being a fireman), I would have had to stay inside the shuttle.

So nothing's perfect, and we've been talking about some real problems that can crop up for people who are way smaller than average. (And, remember, way taller, too.) Still, the ones that have come up so far have been pretty manageable. They don't ruin your life, or even rule it; at the most, they require some adjustments and accommodations here and there. Nothing we've looked at so far is the kind of thing that would keep you from having a happy life, unless you have a burning, passionate desire to sit within ten inches of the steering wheel and no other position will do.

Along with the true limitations and problems

with shortness such as the ones I've been talking about, there are plenty of supposed problems that just aren't real. Some of these were among the ideas that got tossed around in the push to get growth hormones approved for use in short people without a medical problem—the studies that seem to say that short people will be discriminated against and lead miserable, second-class lives. These studies, as you could probably guess, get played up big in the media.

The media loves to take the most eye-popping interpretation of what scientific research says, even if that interpretation is flat-out wrong. So a study that looks at the earnings of tall and short people and suggests that, on average, short people earn less gets a headline like this one that showed up in the *Chicago Sun-Times*: "Long on Earnings; Short Guys Don't Measure Up on Payday"—as if every short guy earns less than every tall guy. Even when the headlines accurately describe what a study seems to say on the surface, the writers can't help but get a dig in. A study that suggested that, on average, people who are taller tend to have higher IQs—a study we'll be talking about in greater depth a little later—was written up in the *Fort Wayne Journal-Gazette* with the headline "Economists Link Height, Smarts." But the stories oversimplified it to the point of insult: One in the *Los Angeles Times* put it this way: "Tall people are smarter than short people." That same story went on to say, "Of course they are. It's easier for them to reach the books on the top shelf at the college library."

You see stuff like this all the time, and it's one more excuse for people to refer to that "Short people got no reason to live" song again. It's enough to make you want to tear your hair out.

Thank goodness it's not true.

The trick, then, is knowing the difference between a real problem and a fake one, and keeping a sense of proportion about it all. And learning to tell what's real from what's hype can save you from a lot of unhappiness. It's the kind of big lesson that each of us has to learn for ourselves.

Why *Me*?

Why are some people short? The question used to drive me crazy.

It's a natural question, and the answers aren't that hard to work out.

In some cases, medical conditions cause people to be short. Some people's bodies don't make the hormones that they need to grow. Others have problems with the heart, lungs, intestines, or kidneys that can prevent them from growing as tall as they might otherwise.

And there are other kids who don't get the nutrition they need when they are small and so their bodies don't take in the building blocks for making as much bone and muscle as they need to reach their full height. That's a common cause of smallness in poor countries, but developed nations such as the United States don't have all that much malnutrition. There are, however, some kids who are malnourished because their parents don't give them the right foods to eat, often by putting them on diets that are unhealthy.

Then there are the people whose bodies keep them from getting the right nutrition. Some have problems with digestion, or have other illnesses that make it hard for them to keep food down or to pull all of the nutrients out of the food that they eat. So illnesses that lead to a lot of vomiting and diarrhea, or that lead a kid to have a poor appetite all the time, can keep someone from reaching his or her full height potential.

Though all of those medical and social conditions exist, they are pretty rare as explanations for being small. The huge, huge majority of people who are short are that way because of genetics: Height is an inherited trait, like brown eyes or red hair or a pug nose.

"The number one cause of short kids is short

parents," says Alice Dreger, the bioethicist at North-western University who has studied height issues.

There's even a scientific term for it: *familial short stature.* It means that a person is short be-cause other members of his or her family are short. There might be members of the family who are taller, sure, but genetics passes out characteristics unevenly. A mother might have blond hair and a father might have brown hair; some of their kids will have brown hair and others will have blond.

It's certainly what happened in my case. For years, I wondered what had happened to leave me a good three inches shorter than any of my brothers, and even a bit shorter than my grandfather, a Russian immigrant who might not have even seen a glass of milk until he got to these shores in his late teens, when he was already fully grown.

I thought that I must have had one of the medi-cal conditions; I'd heard that I was pretty sick for a while when I was just a baby. But when I started work-ing on this book and calling around to members of my family, my mother solved the mystery for me. "Grandma Clara wasn't even five feet!" she told me. "She was little bitty."

Grandma Clara! My father's mother died when I was just ten years old, and I never saw her standing up: she'd been bedridden since having a stroke six years before I was born. I take after Clara in a lot of ways: I have her dark, deep-set eyes with the bags under them. I'm built kind of square, like a pack animal; the old pictures of her show the same boxy body shape. Being short is another one of the genetic traits that I inherited from Clara. Thanks, Grandma!

Each of us is an individual person, but we're also part of larger populations—peoples—who have something in common, such as a nation of origin or an ethnic background. And peoples tend to share traits—some genetic, and some related to the environment. Even though most of a person's height is genetic, there are height traits that groups of people have in common. Americans, and other people in developed nations where nutrition is good, tend to be tall. The tallest people in the world, though, are not the Americans but the Dutch. Men in the Netherlands are, on average, more than six feet tall—six foot one, in fact. Women are, on average, five foot eight. And they are still growing.

The connection between height and nutrition is so strong that the United Nations uses height as a way to measure progress on nutrition in developing countries. It's considered a promising sign that African pygmies, known for being small, have gotten taller over time—though they have some genetic problems that will keep them from getting taller than five feet, according to an article in *The New Yorker* by Burkhard Bilger. For the most part, he wrote, "any population can grow as tall as any other."

What this means for many of us smaller guys is that we may be little because we come from a small-ish people, at least in the current generation. If you're from an immigrant family, chances are that your group is shorter than the American average. The differences tend to balance out over a few generations, though, which is why Bilger says any population can grow as tall as any other. But in your case, if your parents or grandparents came from a country where people tend to be smaller than Americans, your family just might not have had enough generations here in the United States to catch up. You can see that happening in my own family: My short grandmother was born to a family of Russian immigrants, and my short grandfather was born in Russia. I'm short, but a little bit taller than my grandmother was. My children are taller than I am. Their kids might be basketball stars.

There is one more reason that a kid might be short that we haven't discussed: He might not have grown yet. That might seem like a stupid thing to say, but it's actually smart. (You'll find a lot of the things I say are like that.)

One of the biggest mysteries of growth is timing. Doctors can make a fairly good estimate of how tall somebody is going to turn out to be when the kid is at a pretty early age. One of the main methods they use is to take your height at two years and double it. As small as a toddler is, he's still roughly half the height he will reach as an adult. There are more sophisticated ways to do it as well, by comparing a child's height to the height data drawn from many, many other kids, which is basically what the chart in the last chapter was all about.

These methods come up with a rough estimate, with the emphasis on *rough*; my family's pediatrician predicted I'd end up being five foot seven, which is nearly four pretty important inches off the mark. Still, even when the estimate is more accurate, it's missing a vital piece of information. What it can't tell you is *when* you'll reach that full adult height. Because the growth spurt that gets you there can happen just about any time in your adolescence, and you could find yourself reaching average height or better—but just a little later than the kids around you. I was surprised to find out that a good friend of mine at work, David, had been a small kid almost all the way through school. He had been a five-foot, four-inch senior in high school, he confessed, but had a late growth spurt that brought him up to six feet.

It's all part of that bell curve: Most people are destined to end up in the middle, whenever it happens. And the differences in their rates of growth also show up as a bell curve, too, with some growing earlier and some later.

Growing up earlier or later can be a problem for some kids. Julie Graber, a professor of psychology at the University of Florida, works on questions about the timing of growth spurts, which are a major part of going through puberty.

You probably know at least a little bit about puberty by now. You almost certainly know that puberty is the borderline between childhood and adulthood. What everybody knows about puberty is that girls get breasts and boys get deeper voices. But there's a lot more going on. Yes, there are all the changes in sexual equipment and body hair that are on display in the locker room. But the changes work their way through the whole body, through periods of rapid growth that also include a shift from chubby baby bodies to bodies with more lean muscle.

Graber's work focuses on the timing of puberty, which varies—a lot. Though most obvious parts of the process generally kick off around the age of twelve or thirteen, things can begin at ten or even earlier, or start years later than the rest of the group.

Take a look at the charts on page 38, based on ones from the drug maker Eli Lilly. We're not going to do a close reading this time. Instead, just look at the shapes on the chart to get a feel for how much it varies. The charts were also created to show what's called the "velocity" of growth, which is when the spurt starts and ends. Most of the lines are pretty much the same, showing a tight bump on the chart between the ages of twelve and fifteen. But you'll also see two other bumps that are shown in dotted lines. One starts way earlier than the main group, and one starts way later.

Those who ride that first dotted line, the one on the left of the main bump, don't just end up taller than the children around them a year or two early. If they're boys, they look older, too, because they're a little leaner and a little more muscular. Girls who mature early start to "fill out"—developing curvy hips and breasts. Somebody who hits puberty later than the other kids will be relatively smaller, and will still look more babyish.

A lot of what Graber studies is the effect of puberty that begins too early, and she's found some problems associated with it—especially for girls, who are starting to look like women before the other girls around them are. That can lead to some embarrassment and teasing, but it can also open a doorway to the kind of behavior that the early-developing girl might not be emotionally ready to deal with.

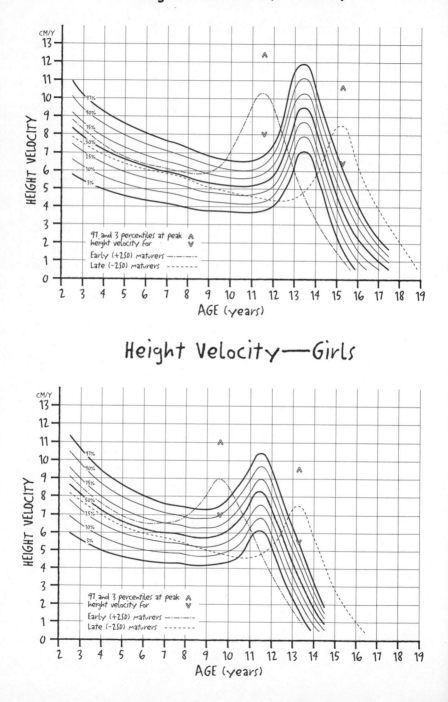

"The individual, mentally, is not necessarily where the body is," Graber said. For girls, that means older boys try to get them to have sex with them before they're ready to weigh the excitement against the big long-term risks and make smart decisions. Graber said, "Being treated as an older individual puts more pressure on youth, and makes bad behaviors more available to them." Studies have shown that this ability to balance long-term risk against short-term fun is something that people grow into over their teen years. The earlier temptations present themselves, the harder it is to take a deep breath instead of just saying, "Why not?"

And so kids who mature early are also likelier to end up trying drugs and alcohol and smoking, she said, and tend to show behavior problems. "Early maturers are getting much more risk," she said. "It's actually protective for a girl to look younger," because she's less likely to get pushed into taking part in activities that might get her into big trouble such as teen pregnancy and drug addiction. Even if these activities don't lead to these huge problems, they can be the kind of distraction from school that eats up hours and drives grades down, limiting options for college later.

Boys who mature early, on the other hand, aren't showing as much of the bad behavior as girls do, she said. Some of the risky behaviors show up with early maturers, but the studies aren't far enough along to show anything solid or big. In fact, she said, boys who get an earlier start on puberty seem to get some benefit from it, and not just a growth spurt that can give them a little confidence.

So with boys, she told me, it's the late maturers who get self-conscious. "If they are not showing changes when other kids are, if they are not as tall, not as developed as somebody else," she said, the late maturers are the ones who are more body conscious and more upset about it. "If you're fourteen years old and a late maturer," she said, "chances are you're shorter than the other kids in your class." Other changes that people don't really think about that come with puberty can cause even subtler differences. Along with the increased lean muscle growth, lungs and heart develop during puberty, she said, so "boys may be feeling a new sense of athleticism that comes from being able to sustain more physical activity and endurance." If you are late to that growth spurt, she said, "you also are likely not getting that surge of muscle development" and athletic ability. The least troublesome situation, she said, is for kids to mature at about the same rate as everybody else does.

So what are we supposed to do about this timing problem, which none of us has any control over? Maybe the best advice comes from baseball great Yogi Berra, whose wisdom is widely quoted for being half Yoda and half Goofy. He once said, "Remember that whatever you do in life, 90 percent of it is half mental." Which is a silly way of saying that your attitude means a lot. If you're one of the early-developing girls and the other girls are making snickering comments about your breasts, well, they'll get theirs. Hang in there, and as they catch up the taunts will fade. And if you're maturing late, it's the same advice: Hang in there. Everybody ends up in the same place, if not the same height. Agonizing didn't help my friend David become a six-footer.

Which brings us back to Yogi: "It's tough to make predictions, especially about the future." (That line hasn't been verified as something Yogi actually said; people have attributed a lot of funny sayings to him that are of questionable origin. Or, as he is supposed to have said, "I didn't say everything I said.")

So there are parts of growth you don't have a lot of control over, except to make things worse for yourself by doing things that keep the body from growing as much as it can. But there are some things that you *can* affect.

How can you make sure to grow as tall as you can, as quickly as you can? The simple answer is to eat right, with healthy meals that include protein (meat, chicken, and stuff like that, though you can also get good protein from sources like soy) and plenty of helpings of fruits and vegetables. Instead of sodas, drink milk, which provides the calcium that goes directly into making those bones. That way you're not preventing your body from getting important building blocks. (Many doctors say that low-fat or even skim milk is a good idea, since it keeps you from taking in unnecessary fat and calories.) All that calcium will help keep those bones from breaking, which is especially important in light of the next thing I'm going to recommend: Exercise. It helps kids reach their full growth potential. The ends of bones have areas called "growth plates" where the new bone is built. Growth plates work better and harder when they take the kind of pounding they get from exercise. That seems to be why so many kids shoot up in the summertime—they are out moving around, and it gets the bones working overtime. That doesn't necessarily mean joining the track team or becoming a defensive lineman—Dance Dance Revolution will do a lot. The important thing is to get out there.

It's like that old slogan for the army: "Be all you can be." You might not be destined to be the tallest kid in the school, or even of average height. But you can do a lot to make sure that you don't miss any opportunities to grow to your full potential. And not just your full potential *height*. Think of Billy, the character in a great old children's book, *The Boy Who Fooled the Giant*. "Maybe I am little," he said, "but I can do big things."

Why Ross Perot Will Never Be President

Of course, the simplest way to counter the notion that short people don't do well in the world is to talk about the ones who do very, very well.

After all, if I were taller, would I work at a better newspaper? Would Ross Perot, the short billionaire who ran for president in 1992 and 1996, have even more billions? Would Michael Bloomberg, the short billionaire who is mayor of New York City, be mayor of a bigger city? No, no, and no.

Okay, neither Ross Perot nor I will ever be president. But somehow I think that height is not the only thing holding us back. That man is a little strange.

This is where something called the focusing illusion comes in. It's an important concept, and a powerful one: It describes the way that many people put too much importance on one aspect of things. People are falling prey to the focusing illusion when they believe a single thing is to blame for their problems—let's say, just for argument's sake, oh, being short—whether it's really the cause of their troubles or not. Alice Dreger explained that somebody who gets teased for being short might come to think that height is the biggest problem in his life and the cause of all his troubles. And parents of short kids might have focusing illusions of their own.

But in fact, there are just a whole lot of short guys out there who do well in every walk of life. And as I was growing up, one of the things that helped me understand that I was going to turn out okay was finding out about them.

I was just a kid in 1969 when the third man to walk on the moon, Pete Conrad, made the trip. As he came down off the ladder of the lunar lander, he made the most famous short-guy joke in the history of the planet. Neil Armstrong, the first man on the moon, had said words some months before that have the ring of history: "That's one step for [a] man, one giant leap for mankind." Now it was Conrad's turn, and at five foot six, he had a different perspective from the lankier Armstrong.

He said, "Whoopee! Man, that may have been a small one for Neil, but that's a long one for me!"

Yuri Gagarin, the first man in space, was even smaller: five foot one.

As I grew up, I collected more and more really successful short guys. The more I learned about their triumphs, the more confident I felt that being the shortest guy I knew did not mean that I was somehow doomed to failure. A lot of short guys do great. Better than great.

Pablo Picasso, at just five feet four, was a giant in modern art. Danny DeVito, a hilarious actor, is five foot two, as is the singer Prince. Spike Lee, the great movie director, is five foot six. Robert Reich, who was labor secretary under President Bill Clinton, stands four foot ten. Not much taller, at just over five feet, is another former aide to Clinton, George Stephanopoulos. He is now the chief Washington correspondent for ABC News and the host of the Sunday talk show *This Week with George Stephanopoulos*. I met him at a party once, and I am proud to say we saw eye to eye.

Speaking of Georges, George Lucas, the creator of *Star Wars*, is five foot six—he must have looked pretty funny standing next to Chewbacca! And Elijah Wood and Sean Astin, who played Frodo Baggins and Sam Gamgee in the Lord of the Rings trilogy, are both five feet six inches as well. Of course, they were playing characters who stood just three feet, six inches tall, so it took special effects to get them to the proper teeny size.

From my childhood to my adulthood, the league of extraordinary short gentlemen were my virtual posse. We were small, but we had stature in the world.

Some of the world's giants were actually pretty small, according to Frank McLynn, a biographer of Napoleon (five and a half feet tall). If your career goal in life is to be a despot, you could do a lot worse than to start small: "Most dictators have been small men," he wrote. "Caesar, Hitler, Mussolini, Stalin, and Franco, as well as Napoleon." Try to tell any of *those* guys that they were doomed to a life of failure because of their height and you'd regret it for the rest of your life. Mercifully, the "rest of your life" would be a very brief amount of time.

Of course, I've heard all the arguments on the other side, too. Like the idea that there are some things that really depend on your being tall enough to compete—like basketball. Right?

Wrong.

Spud Webb played basketball in the NBA from 1985 to 1998, and he's just five feet, six inches.

Muggsy Bogues, another former NBA player, is just five foot three! I love that guy!

So when you see the big headlines about those studies saying that, on average, short people don't achieve as much, or that on average they don't earn as much, or that on average they aren't as smart, there's a handy response:

Who wants to be *average*?

Doom and Gloom

Short people are doomed.

That's the only conclusion you can draw from a quick reading of the media coverage of shortness science. But we're about to do something that most people never do: take a closer, more careful look at the studies and statistics that seem to say that short people are destined to be poor, dumb, and loveless, among other terrible things.

You could be forgiven for hearing some of the studies in the media and thinking that the doom and gloom messages in them are true. I have to admit that before I started doing the research for this book, I actually thought they'd turn out to be true, at least some of them. But as I worked my way back to the original sources of newspaper articles—the original studies, and even the people who conducted the research the studies are based on—I was amazed to see the standard interpretations unravel. And that's what this chapter is about.

Most of the studies that appear to say that being short is a serious, terrible problem have been overinterpreted—either by reporters who are trying to make a more interesting news story and don't take the time to really understand what studies say, or by drug companies to build a case that shortness is a problem that should be treated with their products. When Eli Lilly was telling the government that it should be allowed to sell its growth hormone to kids who were simply small, it presented several PowerPoint slides listing studies that supposedly showed that the short life is pretty awful. Short kids are prone to teasing and bullying and "exclusion," the company told the regulators, and in adulthood they suffer from "social isolation" and a "perception of lower competence"—a fancy way of saying that short kids are left out of the fun and grow up thinking they are a bunch of losers.

And, on a first reading, many of the studies do seem to be saying there are problems ahead. One study seems to suggest, for example, that taller adolescents were the first in their group to get dates.

Now that sounds pretty bad on the romantic front, right? Mrs. Bova, the owner of the store that caters to smaller men, made sure to tell me about the dating study because it had a wrinkle that she really liked. Although taller kids might have started dating earlier than shorter kids overall, another group came out ahead of both: the kids of any height who got to choose their own clothes. And the more short guys care about clothes, the better it could be for her business. . . .

One of the studies that I heard about over and over and over again is about getting jobs, and it seems to suggest that shorter guys lose out. The study, according to most accounts, states that job "headhunters," when given two equally qualified candidates for some hypothetical job—the study apparently even didn't say what kind of job—chose the taller one three out of four times.

I took a closer look. After reading all of the wild claims in newspapers and magazines about what science says, I started hunting down the original studies behind the stories. There are online services and library indexes that help you find such studies, and the jobs study just didn't show up anywhere. The researchers themselves are easy to find online: A Google search turns up just about anybody whose name is attached to a study, and a couple of clicks get an e-mail address.

In my research, I had to weed out a lot of old stuff because, frankly, much of it just isn't very good. Good science tends to be based on results that stand the test of time, and has results that are repeated enough to give us confidence that they are true. When you can't dig up much information on a study in other studies, it's not a good sign for the quality of the science. And what I found, more often than not, was that there wasn't a lot there.

I also found that many of the studies that are frequently mentioned are very old—the height-and-dating study came out in the 1960s, and so did the one about job recruiters—and haven't been confirmed by later work.

I checked in with Stephen Hall, who had gone looking for the headhunter study when he wrote his book. The only mention of it he found was "a one-paragraph item on the front page of the *Wall Street Journal* in 1969." He was not able to find any evidence of the actual study in a respected scientific journal.

Still, so-called studies like that one get passed around without any real challenge or examination. They can be useful to the businesses that have an interest in making shortness seem like a dire problem, so why examine them closely? A sales site for

Shoelifts, which can be slipped into shoes to add a bit of height, posts a news story about one of the studies we'll be discussing. And why not? A little fear might boost their sales, making the cash register go *ka-ching!*

Hall is no fan of the doom-and-gloom studies. A lot of his (and my) skepticism comes from the way that social science research is conducted. The researchers—psychologists and sociologists who study the behavior of people and groups—start out with a hypothesis such as "being short will hurt people in the job market." They then come up with an experiment that will test the hypothesis. In some cases, this is as simple as getting a group of volunteers and asking them how they would respond to a hypothetical situation—such as which person they might hire given two candidates with similar qualifications.

I never did find that study, but I've got an idea of what might have happened—because I have seen the same problem in other behavioral studies. A lot of social science research happens on college campuses, and the data are gathered from college students, who are easy to find and who are encouraged to take part in studies. And while it might be interesting to ask them whether they would be likelier to hire a tall person or a short one, very few college students have much experience hiring anyone at all.

In fact, the most authoritative studies show that height is not a big factor in job interviews. A review of the major studies by Richard Ilkka, a professor of Communication at the University of Wisconsin– Stevens Point, found that there were plenty of body factors that came into play in the real world of job interviews, but height wasn't one of them.

Even when a study seems to show a connection between, say, height and income, the link might not be as simple as it seems. Hall's book pointed out that income might be affected by factors other than height that don't show up in a study—things such as educational background, family history, economic and social background, "and other factors much less easily quantified by yardsticks and dollar signs."

So where's the height penalty we've heard so much about?

That's not to say that all height studies are a load of bunk. The two main studies that suggest there could be some kind of height penalty in income come from respected researchers at some of the most prestigious institutions in the world, and they call for a deeper look.

The best known of the studies linking height to income comes from two economists at the University of Pennsylvania, Andrew Postlewaite and Nicola Persico. They got a tremendous amount of attention when their study first showed up in 2002, because it put hard numbers on height and income. They found that, on average, each additional inch of height was worth $600 per year in increased wages. The differences in income between tall and short people were about the same as differences in income among different races and the differences in income between men and women.

What made the study solid was that it relied on four long-running studies with humongous sets of data. What was even more interesting about the study, though, was that it suggested that height mattered most at age sixteen, and not when the people in the study were fully grown. Tall adults tended to earn more than short adults, but tall adults who were still short at sixteen—maybe because their growth spurt came late, for example—earned less. And the short adults who had been above-average height at age sixteen but ended up short still earned as if they were tall.

So I called up Andrew Postlewaite, who said that he and Dr. Persico, along with the graduate student who helped them on the study, Dan Silverman, "were short as teenagers." "None of us is tall now," he added. He is five foot eight.

Dr. Postlewaite was quick to hit the point that, as the science guys say, "correlation is not causation." Just because the averages suggest that someone shorter will earn less doesn't mean that shorter stature is the *cause* of earning less. And something that looks like a link might be less than it seems.

He told me that this is a message that he taught to his own kids with a funny comparison. He said that there is a "near perfect correlation" between the number of Baptist ministers in a city and the number of murders in the city. "But the solution isn't to kill all the Baptist ministers," he said. Big cities just have more crime than small towns, and more churches, too. Things may show up in a study together, but that doesn't mean that one causes the other, and it doesn't mean that being short means you, as an individual, will necessarily make less money than anybody else.

Dr. Postlewaite and Dr. Persico also suggest that their study says another very interesting thing: If there is a difference in pay between tall people and short people, it's not prejudice against short guys that's at the root of it. Otherwise, height at the age of sixteen would make no difference. It would all be about how tall you were when you started interviewing for jobs. So instead, they believe their study shows that the real problem is self-image.

But that message is a little subtle, and gets lost. Instead what you get are headlines like this one that showed up in the *Chicago Sun-Times*: "Long on Earnings; Short Guys Don't Measure Up on Payday."

And there was another part of the study that didn't get a lot of attention, Postlewaite told me. The height advantage in income disappeared for the shorter kids who got involved in athletics or other school activities. That kind of stuff, he suggested, must set up a sense of well-being and belonging that boosts your chances in life. It's a concept that economists call human capital.

"The message to short people is they have to realize that there's a benefit to doing these things," Dr. Postlewaite told me. "If they're too short for basketball [doesn't he know about Spud Webb?], they should push themselves to get involved with the newspaper or the yearbook," he said, or in sports such as wrestling, in which smaller people can shine.

So the most famous study that says height means wealth doesn't really say that. One down, one to go.

The other really famous study that recently came out is by Anne Case and Christina Paxson at Princeton University. That one, which appeared in the summer of 2006, set off an even bigger storm. Case and Paxson agreed with the Penn guys that tall people, as a group, tend to earn more than short guys, and are more likely, on average, to be executives. But, using much of the same data as Postlewaite and Persico, they came up with a completely different explanation. As they wrote in their paper, "On average, taller people earn more because they are smarter."

Whoa.

Well, you can imagine the headlines—I already mentioned my personal favorite, "Economists Link Height, Smarts." And you can imagine the reaction. When I reached Anne Case on the phone, she told me stories about getting hate mail and crank calls after her study came out. "Some of them really were obscene," she said. "I stopped writing letters back to people, because they were so angry."

Like Dr. Postlewaite, she said that a lot of the stories that came out about the research got the message wrong. The study, she explained, was not about how tall somebody is as an adult, but how tall they are at a very young age and what that says about their later development. Dr. Paxson and Dr. Case used measurements of their subjects at the age of three—before school comes into the picture at all, and well before the magic age of sixteen that Dr. Postlewaite and Dr. Persico were talking about. "As early as age three—before schooling has had a chance to play a role—and throughout childhood, taller children perform significantly better on cognitive tests," they wrote.

Dr. Paxson and Dr. Case, you see, are specialists in nutrition and development, and they were hoping to get the word out that the most important thing is to ensure children receive the care and food they need from the mother's pregnancy into their youth to make sure that they reach their full potential—and height is just the most obvious way to measure those good practices.

Someone whose genetics were going to limit him to being five feet, six inches and reaches his full height would probably turn out smarter than a guy who is five foot ten but who would have topped out at six foot three if he had gotten better nutrition. The financial fortunes of the shorter population are dragged down, she said, by the fact that a larger number of people in that group may have been stunted by disease, poor nutrition, and some of the other things that make people smaller than they would be otherwise. As their paper put it, "environmental factors that are thought to influence cognitive development" also affect height. Correlation, sure, but not causation.

So, she said, the key issue of her study is smarts, not height. Even though the people with smarts, or "good cognitive function," as the term goes, tended to be the taller ones, anybody who showed good cognitive function earned the same in adulthood whether they were tall or short. "The difference disappears," she said. "For people who did well in cognitive tests in early, early childhood, it doesn't matter how tall they are" as adults "when it comes to earning ability."

Roll that one around in your head for a while: The author of the study just completely undercut the sound-bite message that the media took from it. "There's no systematic relationship between height and earnings," she said, once you put everyone whose intelligence tests at age five are similar on an equal footing. So a study that uses much of the same data as Dr. Postlewaite and Dr. Persico did, and that was held out as the worst kind of news for short guys, actually turns out to be the best news of all. If a person who is short is well nourished and intelligent, he won't lose out in earnings—whatever his height, and whether or not he builds "human capital" in sports and clubs.

So maybe now you're asking, "What if I'm short AND dumb?"

Well, you're not. You've read this far, haven't you?

Once you take a closer look at studies, there's not much doom or gloom. A lot of the studies that get tossed around aren't based on solid work, and even the best ones that suggest a statistical correlation between height and income are a little fuzzy when it comes to proving that height is the cause. And as rich short guys such as Ross Perot and Michael Bloomberg prove, averages aren't destiny.

You can become a science sleuth yourself, and arm yourself for future studies. Put on your skeptic's hat and ask the tough questions. Any time you read about a study in the newspaper or online, you should ask yourself what the possible sources of bias are. *Bias*, in everyday language, is prejudice. But in studies, it means the factors that can cause research to come up with inaccurate results—such as asking a bunch of college students about their hiring preferences. Here are a few examples.

Sample size bias generally involves studying a group that's too small to let you draw broad conclusions about the general population.

Selection bias comes from studying people who aren't necessarily like the general population. A lot of the studies about whether short kids suffer because of their small size focus on kids who show up at clinics to seek growth hormone treatment. They are, in other words, the most likely people to feel that being short is a huge burden, and they can make the situation look worse than it is for the general population.

Drop-out bias happens when you study things such as how well a drug works but you don't account for the number of people who stop taking the drug during the course of the study. Since the people dropping out are the ones who are likeliest to have not seen much benefit from the drug, or to have had the worst side effects, the group that remains are the ones likelier to say that the drug is really great.

Reporting bias is the result of asking people who have an interest in a certain outcome to report on that outcome. For example, if you ask a bunch of parents who just paid a lot of money to give their kids hormone injections whether the injections are improving their child's life, they are likely to want to believe that it the shots are helping, and that might affect their answers. A more reliable study would come up with ways to measure the child's quality of life without asking the parents.

Keep the question of bias in mind as we look at some of the flaws in other studies—the ones that say short kids are miserable. Those studies, too, look a little different up close and under a strong light.

Take David Sandberg, a psychologist at the University of Michigan who has studied the psychology of being short. His work over more than ten years has shown the shortcomings, so to speak, of the doom-and-gloom studies about the effects of being short on self-esteem and mental health.

He points out that even though there are studies that suggest kids were upset and anxious about their height, the studies were drawn from kids who had gone to clinics seeking treatment. That's the selection bias I just mentioned. The families that showed up at clinics were the people who felt very, very strongly that being small was a big problem, he told me.

Dr. Sandberg's research, on the other hand, says that short kids generally do just fine. In a paper that was published in 1994, he interviewed all the kids who came into an endocrinology clinic in Buffalo, New York—more than 550 of them between 1990 and 1997. This wasn't just asking college students questions. He was talking to the short kids directly, at the time that they and their families were seeking help.

Yeah, sure, the short kids reported being teased—more than half of them, actually. And the way they were treated caused some stress in their lives. But—and this is the cool part of the study— they were *dealing with it*. Only a few of the kids in the study reported having serious problems, he said.

He knew this in his gut, he told me in an interview. When he surveys kids who come into doctors' offices, he said, "you find they are *not* basket cases— far from it." And in the broader population, the effect is nowhere to be found, he said.

He published an even more interesting study in 2004. This time he took on the notion that other people see short people as having problems. Instead of using the kids who had been driven to clinics, he tried testing his theories out in the general population. He and his helpers asked hundreds of kids in the Buffalo area to choose their classmates for roles in a school play, with the parts being defined by phrases like "a good leader," "gets picked on," "is shy," and "gets left out."

There was no play—the idea was to trick the kids into revealing their attitudes about height without actually talking about whether their classmates were tall or short. The researchers checked out who got picked for what. And Dr. Sandberg's results were—again—startling. If being short means lower social status, you would have seen the little guys picked for the troubled roles. But the only perception about the smaller students was that they were likely to be thought of as "younger looking" than the other kids—and the researchers found that "the social repercussions of being perceived as young were of minimal significance."

In another part of his study, Dr. Sandberg asked students to name their friends. If short people are truly socially isolated, it would show up. But he found a different result: "Short kids were as likely to have tall friends as tall kids," he said.

In fact, not only did they find no real problem with being short but, he wrote, "the present findings indicate that there is little benefit to being tall."

When he described the findings to me in an interview, he said, "This was totally unexpected." Height didn't affect the number of friends the kids had, or the height of those friends. It had nothing to do with how well students were liked by others, what the others thought of them, or even of their own perception of their reputation within the school. In other words, bupkis.

Julie Graber, the researcher in Florida who studies the problems of early puberty and late puberty, said that even though some problems have shown up for the late-maturing boys—they show more "depressive symptoms," she said—they are not showing "serious problems" overall. Her research shows a bump-up in problems as they reach adulthood, around nineteen or twenty years old, but it's not clear why, she said, and suggested that it might be the "sleeper effect" of kids who matured late finally trying some of the things that got their early-maturing classmates in trouble in earlier years. But studies like this show what's happening without really explaining why it happens, she said. "We're pushing ourselves to see what the 'why' is," she said.

Dr. Graber said she wonders whether the studies even mean what they seem to, especially when data collected by economists is used to show something as personal as self-esteem. "We have a pretty good sense that height is measured well," she said, but adds, "If you're talking about something like self-esteem, do we know whether it is measured particularly well?" You can't just hold up a yardstick to self-esteem. And is income really the best way to measure success in life, when many people with wonderful careers don't get rich?

I don't mean to say that individual people don't have stress or problems because they're short. I know how I yearned to be bigger when I was a kid.

But what I am saying is that there's no evidence that being short is a terrible problem for people or that it predicts a second-rate life for us. You don't *have* to be psychologically burdened by being short.

It ultimately comes down to how you handle things—how *you* deal with being short, or being different in any way.

Bullies

One night at the roller skating rink, back when I was in high school, a guy decided to give me a hard time. I had never met him before, but he started rolling up behind me and bumping his skates into mine so that I'd stumble and have to wave my arms wildly to regain my balance. I wasn't a very good skater, so I must have looked pretty ridiculous. He kept doing it, and for good measure gave me a couple of shoves.

I probably don't need to mention that he was taller than I was, right? I looked like a guy he could knock around to feel big, and to entertain his friends.

He was making me madder and madder. I had done nothing to this jerk, and he was trying to humiliate me! Even worse, he was succeeding! I was also scared—before long, I was going to fall hard, and that was going to hurt. So I started out confused: *Why me?* And moved pretty quickly into fear: *I'm going to end up breaking my wrists! I'm going to bust my head open!* But it wasn't many shaky circuits of the rink before those emotions were finally pushed aside by anger. I had been bullied too many times, and I was really tired of it.

I stopped skating. I turned around to face the guy, shaking a little.

"Cut it out!" I shouted. I think there were some cuss words in there, too, but you get the idea. "If you want to fight," I said, "we can go outside."

I was scared to death, but for once my voice didn't crack. The guy jeered and said, "I ain't gonna fight *you*," as if I wasn't worth his trouble.

And he skated away. And he left me alone for the rest of the night.

Lesson: I didn't let him make being short a problem for me. And he gave up.

I met plenty of bullies as I made my way through childhood. They tended not to be very bright, and tended to pick on people smaller than they were. They do this for the same reason that baboons rarely take on prey more than one fifth their own weight:

Under the bluster, they are cowards. It took me a long time to learn to stand up to them.

According to a recent study, 90 percent of kids in third to sixth grades say they have been bullied. (Since we've been talking about what makes a study trustworthy, let me just say that this one was done by researchers at a reputable institution, by the Stanford University School of Medicine, and funded by the National Institutes of Health, and was published in a well-regarded place: the *Journal of Developmental and Behavioral Pediatrics*. It was based on surveys of 270 kids at three schools in California and Arizona. That doesn't mean it's perfect—I'd like to see more kids surveyed from a broader area—but it's a good start.)

There's a bully—at least one—in every school. And in just about every TV show about school (Hello, Nelson Muntz!). And in just about every comic strip (like the near-caveboy, Moe, in *Calvin and Hobbes*).

Why are they such a big part of popular culture? Because they're such a big part of our lives. Stephen Hall, the author of *Size Matters,* told me that when he gives speeches about his book, he usually asks the middle-aged men in his audience to raise their hands if they remember "both the first and last names of the guys who tormented them" back in their school days.

"Virtually everybody's hand goes up," he said.

I had my share. In elementary school, a kid named Alford made the school bus a miserable experience. He used to sit behind me and spit small pieces of glass at the back of my neck. I mean, who *spits glass*? He was tough.

Luckily, my older brothers watched out for me. One day, my brother Dick, three years my senior and a lot bigger, climbed onto the school bus and asked the driver to stop for a minute. He said, real loud, "Who's Alford?" Dick, who has always been a very gentle guy, looked fierce. Nobody said anything. He looked around and then said, "Johnny Schwartz is my brother. If you're going to mess with him, you're going to have to start with me."

That solved the problem with Alford. But in middle school, it started up again. New school, new bullies. They hit me up for lunch money, or just picked on me because they were bored. I remember one guy in PE, Gordy, used to give me knocks on the back of my head. Out of nowhere: *Thwock. Thwock. Thwock.* He was tall and strong, and I took the harassment quietly until I couldn't stand it anymore. One day during gym, when we were sitting in the bleachers and he knocked me, I reached back and tried to hit him as hard as I could.

Superman fantasies only get you so far. My swing was wild and weak; I ended up tapping him on the shin. He grabbed me by the neck and pushed my head down between the slats of the bleachers and bounced it around with a *thumpeta-thumpeta* rhythm. Mr. Liberato, the coach, finally noticed the fight and broke it up. "What's this about?" he demanded to know.

Gordy, trying to look innocent, said, "He attacked me!"

The coach laughed out loud.

As the study about bullying showed, I was not alone. And Eli Lilly, the drug company, argued that bullying was one of the big reasons that the FDA should approve the use of their drug for kids who were merely small.

But wait.

If 90 percent of kids are bullied, that means bullying happens to just about everyone, tall or short. That's why all the hands go up in Steve Hall's audience, right?

I asked a tall person what he thought of all this. Dan Barry is a friend of mine from the newspaper, and one of the best reporters and writers I've ever met. He told me that he was tall for his age all the way through school on Long Island in New York State, but he was still the target of bullies.

Why was Dan singled out? For one thing, he went to parochial school, which meant he wore a uniform that included dark green pants, a blazer, a white button-down shirt, and a tie that was either green or plaid. Dressed in what he called this "parochial school clown outfit," he remembered, "you're basically asking to be beat up, in a way," he said.

Another reason he thinks he got picked on was that he never ran away from a bully—and, he acknowledges, "I could have been a little bit of a smartass." But for all he knew, he might have gotten kicked around because he was a voracious reader—one day he was reading as he went up the stairs, and another kid started pummeling him.

Whatever the reason, the result, he remembered, was pain. In his wonderful book *Pull Me Up*, he talked about the school bus, which was a daily dose of hazing, with seniors ordering the underclassmen around and humiliating them, piling books on freshmen's arms and, if they dropped one, slapping them around.

Lots of people got picked on, he told me one day when we were talking about his childhood, and for lots of stupid reasons. "You could be picked on for being overweight. You could be picked on because you had acne. You could be picked on because you were short. You had braces. Your nose was perceived to be a little longer, or your hair stuck up in a funny way," he said. "Or that you had freckles, or because your father was the janitor, or because everyone knew your father was an alcoholic, or because your parents would fight and people could hear it." As he went down the list, he seemed to be mentally calling up the faces of the kids he grew up with who fit each description.

David Sandberg (the researcher at the University of Michigan) said that Dan has it exactly right. "Everybody gets teased," he said. For someone of normal height, the insults might change from day to day. "One day you'll be called gay—the next day you'll be called a jerk," he said. "It's easy for that person not to take it seriously."

But, on the other hand, if someone is short, then the bullies are likely to focus on height. "If you're short, the likelihood is that you're going to be teased about something that's factually accurate," Sandberg said. "And that might sting."

Not giving in to the focusing illusion isn't easy. But it's important. Being short, or being too tall, or too whatever is only as big a problem as we let it be.

Growing Up Short:
A User's Guide

So how does a person walk tall? By refusing to be small.

If this book is about anything, it's that each of us can resist the self-image that others try to force on us—the one that says "loser." It is a matter of attitude, and attitude is largely a matter of developing strong habits of thinking.

After all, most people survive the teasing and the bullying of childhood—it might upset us, but it usually doesn't kill us. My buddy Dan said something about bullying that a lot of people say about the things that make them miserable: "It builds character."

That sounds terrible, right? Sappy and inspirational, like one of those posters in the gym. But it's true. I found that any time I stood up to a bully, like the creep in the roller rink, he would leave me alone. And after Gordy banged me around that day, we got to be pretty friendly. When I called him on the phone decades later, he even told me that he had stepped in to keep another guy from taking my lunch money in junior high—something I hadn't known at the time. "I told him you were my friend," he said.

You've probably figured out that this is all leading up to more talk about the focusing illusion. I'm not saying that being short—or freckle-faced or whatever—is fantastic or wonderful, or that there are no problems associated with it. But this chapter is about putting the problems in their place and talking about how to get a sense of proportion.

All of us have problems—adolescence can be a miserable time, for a whole lot of reasons. Your body is changing, you're clumsy and clueless a lot of the time. The social networks at school are baffling and, except for a few really lucky kids, dating is just a cruel joke.

The kids around me were starting to date way back in middle school. The tall guys like Paul, with his exotic looks and his great sense of humor, could ask pretty much anybody out. There was a girl I really liked in eighth grade, and we talked a lot and kissed some, but I didn't start dating anyone seriously until high school. Nothing until then seemed to click. And it felt like everybody was dating but me.

When I got my first serious girlfriend, she was somebody I met on a school trip, and she lived twenty-five miles away. She was funny and red-headed and liked me, too, and when I asked her if we could get together again, she actually said yes!

That was the year I got my driver's license, and I found out just how fast a Buick Skylark could make the trip between Galveston and Dickinson. I didn't break the sound barrier, but I might have broken the bank if I'd ever gotten stopped for speeding.

So why did I have to go twenty-five miles to get a girlfriend? At the time, of course, I was sure it was because I was so short. But looking back, it might have had less to do with my small size than with my big mouth. I was a pretty obnoxious kid in a small town, and by the time the kids in my age group were starting to date, we all knew each other very well. A good friend of mine, Yolanda, told me after we were grown up that back when we were kids, she had thought I was stuck up. By the time I was a teenager,

I was a lot easier to get along with, but the kids I grew up around probably didn't see that at the time—we had long memories, and long grudges, too. So heading over to another town let me meet people who hadn't seen that side of me.

Go with what works, I say.

At the end of my junior year in high school, a great girl, Cathleen, moved into my town from Austin. She was artsy: She wore leotards and blue jeans to school and dyed her hair black. She was instantly picked for the lead role in every school play. And she hadn't known me during those earlier, obnoxious days.

The focusing illusion does short people the favor of simplifying the problems to a single, obvious cause: being short. That's how it ties people down—by providing a convenient excuse for problems, the focusing illusion keeps them from realizing what other issues they might have that could be fixable. It can keep people from reaching their full potential, and it can also keep them from trying new things. If you assume that all of your problems have been the result of your size, then you can only assume it will get in the way again. And so it keeps you from recognizing opportunities that might be out there.

I could have let the focusing illusion hold me back and let myself give up before I even asked Cathleen out. I could have assumed that being short would come into play no matter what, and I'd get brushed off. But I didn't. I was still pretty short, but my personality had grown. And it made all the difference. We had a great senior year together.

Kids aren't the only ones who suffer from the focusing illusion. Dr. Rogol, the epidemiologist who's skeptical about giving growth hormone to kids who are merely short, said parents too are quick to blame the most obvious thing when their children have troubles. The fact is, a substantial number of people in the world have behavioral problems and even mental illness. The parents of short kids with problems, he said, tend to think that small size is a big part of the reason.

Dr. Rogol told me that he occasionally gets calls that strike him as bizarre. One mother whose kid was actually normal height called to ask for hormone shots "because the college tennis coaches said he would be a much better player if he were taller."

Dr. Rogol sounded pretty upset as he told me the story, and remembered getting pretty rude with her on the phone. He never heard from her again, and figured that she found somebody else to give her son the shots.

Dr. Sandberg said that when a short kid is brought to a doctor like Rogol because he's having behavior problems in school, the parents might assume that the kid is having a hard time because he is short. But, Dr. Sandberg told me, he suspects that giving the kid hormones is not necessarily going to help him improve his behavior or grades. "I can think of many other reasons that the child could be unhappy and doing poorly in school," he said. By making size the whole problem and more height the only solution, it's possible to miss more important issues that are causing trouble, he said.

With the drug companies pushing hormone therapy as a way to buy height, many parents have become convinced, he said, that the answers to their kids' problems all come down to height and that they can be fixed with shots. It's the same kind of thinking that has led doctors and parents to look to drugs such as Ritalin as a simple, quick fix for behavior problems.

Dr. Dreger, the bioethicist at Northwestern University, said hormone therapy is a weird version of what she calls "the American way of parenting," which she explained is "all about consumption" and "getting your kid everything you can get them"— whether it's the best preschool, the tutoring, or the sports equipment. "Parents feel they are not good parents if they don't get their kids every medical intervention they can."

The problem, she said, is that medical treatments "don't make you better. In many cases they make you sicker." If she learned anything from her work with families of kids with birth defects, she said, it's "don't sweat the small stuff."

Dr. Dreger said that many short parents had a hard time growing up short and want to save their kids from the emotional turmoil that comes from not measuring up. "They think of the worst things they ever suffered and hope their kids won't go through that," she said. It's a natural impulse that goes along with wrapping foam around every edge of every sharp corner so that a toddler doesn't bump his head too hard on the coffee table. But what these parents don't think about, she said, is that "they all made it. Many of them would be able to say, 'I emotionally benefited from this challenge.'" Like Dan said: It builds character.

Dr. Sandberg has a lot to say about all this. It was his research with the clever trick of asking kids to cast a play, you'll remember, that did so much to show that being short does not cause serious psychological problems and doesn't make other kids see you in a demeaning light.

When I talked with Dr. Sandberg about his research, he went back to a notion we touched on before: Being short might not be such a huge deal in the grand scheme of things. He said that his work really undercuts the idea that short kids need the hormones to keep from suffering the psychological problems that come from being short. "It always used to be said that these children are victimized," he said, and "don't adapt" to being short.

If that were true, he said, those psychological problems would show up in the testing that he does before they start treatment. But it doesn't. "If you do a proper study, you don't see a difference," he said, even in the kids who show up at clinics—and these are the ones who would be most likely to show the problems. They might want to be taller, as many people do. But their height isn't causing them deep psychological stress.

None of this kind of thinking, however, has stopped the hormone steamroller. Dr. Sandberg wrote in the play-acting study that his study "provides little support for the notion that extremes of stature, either short or tall, serve as a risk factor for poor social adjustment among youths in the general population." So, he warned in the paper, don't base decisions on using growth hormone "in assumptions regarding the presumed psycho-social stresses" from being short.

After showing through all of his work that the psychological stresses are not so great, he said, "What you're left with is the stereotype that it sucks to be short." Even then, he said, it's easy enough for a parent to go for the hormones, thinking, *what is the problem with taking something that will make you taller?*

In fact, he wrote, more caution is called for

when it comes to the push to expand the use of hormones. Making the drugs more broadly available and recommending them for kids who are merely short makes all the stereotypes that say there's something wrong with being short sound as if they're true. Amazingly, he's saying that short kids don't suffer today, but they *might* have problems down the road if the use of growth hormone becomes more common and society expects people to use hormones and get bigger.

Stephen Hall knows a lot about frustrations that come from being short. His book helps sort through what's solid and what's bogus in the world of short science. I asked if we could get together and talk.

We sat outside in Bryant Park in New York City. It's a funny place, that park, in the middle of midtown Manhattan. The city is rushing, rushing, rushing everywhere around you, but for the time you're in the park everything is relaxed. And we sat down to talk on the kind of spring day so beautiful that it makes you want to stay outside as long as possible. People walked by, all shapes and sizes— eating, hanging out with buddies from their offices, lying out on the grass to feel the sun all over.

Hall was very small growing up, he recalled, and even now has grown into only the fifth percentile of adults at about five feet, six inches—taller than I am, but still little. To him, the important thing was that he was very little when he was in his teen years. "Being much smaller in my childhood seemed to make an enormous difference," he said, and it can be an emotional issue for others, too.

In the book, he talks about being upset about being so small. "All it does is gets you to think of all the things that might be wrong with you," he said.

But while Hall believes that height is important psychologically, and draws on his on experience of misery, he does a great job of reading the studies and realizing that, ultimately, it's not such a big deal. Kids in school form alliances, and height is not the biggest factor in how those alliances come together. Acceptance changes fifty times a day, he said. Some kids accept you, but you don't really accept them. "Nothing is predestined," he said. Size isn't the only thing that controls social acceptance.

But, he said, the studies and the narrow, sensationalistic interpretations of them are still out there. "People see these sound bites and headlines and get concerned about it. And it's not the case."

Now, I don't mean to say that short guys don't have stress or problems because of their size. It would be awfully dumb of me to argue that averages don't necessarily have an effect on individuals when it comes to things like income, and then try to tell people that they can't have psychological problems over being short since most people don't. And neither would Hall.

In our conversation in the park, Hall said that size is an important part of our emotional baggage— but even he wouldn't go so far as to say that small size is the most critical component of it. Or, as he put it in his book, "It matters, yes, but it's not the only thing that matters."

He spent a lot of his childhood waiting for a growth spurt that he now calls "too little and too late." And he admits that there was a fair amount of focusing illusion at work in his unhappiness. He was convinced that it was being short that made him feel like an outsider, and not his glasses, or his braces, or his braininess, or the fact that he was new in town, or the fact that adolescence is a time when it's pretty normal to feel frustrated and alone. He called that time an "existential wasteland."

Isn't that a great phrase, *existential wasteland*? It conjures the whole idea of an existence that's kind of bleak, and it does describe what adolescence is like for a lot of people. And it's true, everybody has something to be upset about in this existential wasteland.

One of my good friends from high school, Gregg Lambdin, tells me that he was miserable all through his own adolescence because he was . . . tall.

Gregg shot up in middle school. He is six feet, six

inches today, or one foot and three inches taller than I am. Gregg was huge, even back then. "Do you remember the old adage 'Act your age and not your shoe size'?" he asked me. "When I was thirteen, I wore size thirteen shoes." And he got teased for it. "My friends would make fun of my long feet. They'd call them banana boats or flippers. It was very awkward," he said. "I just felt kind of grotesque, you know?" He was taller than both of his parents. He remembers walking with a slouch so he wouldn't stand out as much. "My mom was telling me constantly to stand up straight," he remembered. She would give him a sharp tap between the shoulder blades. "'Stand up straight! Stand up straight!' she'd say."

He got tired of hearing the same jokes over and over. "How's the weather up there?" For several years, he worked in a hospital as a nurse and saw fifty patients a night. Every night, he says, he could count on somebody asking "How tall are you? Did you ever play basketball?" He used to think to himself, *If I hear that one more time, I'm going to scream.*

He's a quiet and serious guy, but he seems even more serious when he says, "People have this false notion that it's a plus—it's great to be tall. And I say, 'What? What's so great about it?'"

He had some of the same problems with the bell curve that short kids have; only he was on the other side. Just like the short guys, he has a hard time finding clothes that fit well, and the measured world sometimes leaves him out. Long airplane rides can be agony, with his knees jammed against the seat in front of him and his back crammed against the seat. He often gets off of planes with a backache and sore legs.

"There were cars I wanted and couldn't buy," he said. "I sat in a Corvette and I couldn't use the steering wheel! My knees were locked on either side of the wheel." Today he drives a "tiny little car," a BMW Z4, because even though it's small, it was designed to be comfortable for a big person to drive.

But his problems were the worst in his teen years, he told me. He thought he'd try to make something of his height, he remembered, trying out for basketball. But it was awful. He was awkward, and the other guys on the team gave him even more trouble about that. They'd yell, "You're really *sorry*!' and "Oh, man, if I were as tall as you are, I'd be really great."

Then he tried out for track and the high jump, and everything changed. He found he could jump— by the tenth grade, he set a national record for his age group, and there was a story about it in the *Galveston Daily News*. Debbie, one of our friends, baked him a cake and brought it into school the next day to celebrate. It had a high bar on it, and said "Congratulations from your friends."

He remembered, "When I saw that, I almost cried. It made me feel I was part of the group." He was building what Andrew Postlewaite, the economist who studied height and income, called "human capital."

Ultimately, then, his height paid off. "At this point I'm perfectly happy with it—I'm pleased with the way I turned out," he said. "But at that time, I was quite miserable."

Many of us just don't seem to like our bodies much, whether we're short or tall, fat or scrawny. Dr. Roberto Olivardia is an expert at Harvard University in something called body imaging and body dysmorphic disorder, a complicated term that basically means not having a realistic or happy relationship with your body.

At the extremes, the problems with body imaging lead to life-threatening conditions such as anorexia, so it's serious stuff. An anorexic person, for example, sees a fat person in the mirror even if the body is actually thin to the point of wasting away. Dr. Olivardia works mainly with people on the severe end of things, and he says there are plenty of things that people hate about their bodies—their hair, arms, nose—and, of course, their height. Being short is "one of the few things about our bodies that we can't control at all, even through cosmetic surgery," he told me. "I've worked with men who, if they didn't like their nose, they got a nose job," or got liposuction or stomach surgery to lose weight. He also works with boys and men who take bodybuilding to a dangerous level, including the use of steroids.

According to him, people who are most troubled by being short, he said, tend to see their size as part of their "masculine gender identity." Men who are upset over being short, he said, worry that they are "viewed as weak, as not virile." They agonize over the idea that "people look at them as little boys as opposed to men."

It's not as if we come up with these messages all on our own, he said. "The media, for the most part, really promotes—especially for adolescents—a way to look and to dress and to act." At the moment we are naturally the most self-conscious, movies and TV undercut us even more.

And when people try to console teenagers over these feelings, he said, they often say exactly the wrong thing. Nothing's worse than having someone tell you that looks aren't important. "That's not true! We live in a culture where looks are incredibly important," he said. "Should they be? That's another question."

Sometimes, he acknowledged, size really *is* an

issue. One of his patients was actually told indirectly that a company he was trying to get a job with wanted someone taller. A potential manager who turned him down for the job said, "We want to communicate a sense of strength, a sense of firmness in our employees," and that they required employees to have "certain characteristics" that express that strength. The patient, of course, was stunned. He asked, "You're not hiring me because of my *height?*" And the would-be boss backed off and said there were other issues and qualifications.

But even the short people who don't get so blatant a message, Olivardia said, "feel that people are seeing them that way [even though] most of the time they are not."

Occasionally, one of Dr. Olivardia's patients will bring up the studies such as the Penn paper about height and income. ("I can't tell you how many people bring up that study!" he told me, with a little frustration.) He responds by asking his patients to take the headlines with a grain of salt. He points out that "there are many scientific studies— some are good, some are not good. Sometimes newspaper and TV shows pick up something that sounds sexy, that sounds interesting, without really looking at the scientific methodology of the study" to see if it stands up. But even if a study shows a trend, he said, "that's not destiny."

Whether or not a short person gets discriminated against in a serious way, Dr. Olivardia said, anyone smaller than average can expect to be the object of jokes and occasional rejection. Somebody, somewhere, will make a stupid comment about your height, or a girl will turn you down for a date because she only likes tall guys. When such things happen, he explained, "how you deal with that—how you respond to it—makes a difference."

He said, "The [key] is not to deny that it happens, but to say, 'What do we do about it?'"

If a comment or a joke leaves you feeling humiliated or wounded, he said, that person has tried to exercise a little power over you, to be dominant. He compares it to the way dogs in a pack have to submit to the alpha dog. The risk is that you take the insult to heart, "internalizing" it and ending up feeling that you're not good enough. From there, he said, "you start to act that role," being less assertive and walking with your head down and your thoughts dark.

"Thinking, 'If only I were taller' generates no return for you," he said. "It's like going into quicksand." And there's no reason to let these things hit you hard. "The notion that one comment can destroy or devastate someone's self-esteem—you cannot give somebody that power," he said. "You have to go about attacking those thoughts."

And so, he said, he encourages his patients to say, "I'm going to take my power back. I'm going to be the one in control." How? "You can take your power back by having something to say, or realizing that one person shouldn't have that amount of power over your life." He tells his patients that there are short people who are happy and tall people who are not. He encourages them to have a quick response ready for the lame jokes.

Beyond snappy comebacks, he said, everyone, short or tall, needs an "anchor . . . something you feel good about." That could be your friendships, or sports, or your creativity, or your ability to get up and make a speech or tell a joke. With an anchor, he said, the things like insults that hit all of us aren't so hard to take. "It's not like you're not going to be affected by it," he said. But "you're anchored in. You're going to sway a little, to and fro, but it's not going to unravel you." In other words, everybody takes a knock now and then, but people with good anchors can recover. "It's the difference between being upset that somebody said something to you and being devastated by it," he said.

Hall said part of what helped him get over his anxiety about being small was wrestling, for which size is not as important as strength, which you can build, and moves, which you can learn. He never won a varsity match, he said, but won his junior varsity matches. He recalled it all as "a terrific experience," though he also remembered it as humiliating. "Much as I hated it," he wrote, "wrestling probably saved my adolescence. Being on a team is a form of belonging. The camaraderie was not only a kind of tonic but also a form of social vaccination." Nobody picked on him after he joined the wrestling team, he wrote, and "being even marginally proficient at something athletic conferred on me a certain amount of self-esteem."

And here's a bold thought. What if being short helps us in some way? Hall told me that trouble, in moderate doses, is a great teacher. "Although being shorter than average carries with it a considerable amount of tribulation and challenges in childhood and especially adolescence," he said, "it should be a huge advantage once you reach adulthood."

Say what?

He's serious.

From childhood on, he said, small people "are forced to learn they can't get their way by sheer physical means." It starts with something as simple as not being big enough to grab the toys they want away from the other kids and get away with it. This is an important lesson that many bigger kids don't learn until much later, if ever.

Not being able to muscle your way across the playground, he said, sets up what he calls "subtle pressure on smaller kids to cultivate other ways of exercising their will," whether that means becoming verbally quick and persuasive or developing a good sense of humor. It could also help people to develop greater empathy (the ability to better understand the feelings of others).

These traits, he argued, "turn out to be enormously useful social skills" later in life—on the job, and even in romance. In the right proportions, they add up to that elusive quality called charm. When I asked him if that's how he won his wife, who is several inches taller than he is, he looked a little sheepish and chuckled. But he didn't deny it.

"Dealing with adversity, having exposure to adversity early on, is very useful in how someone goes through his life," Hall said. You become wiser, and in a weird way, he said, you might be "inoculated" against stress by having to deal with it early on, just as a vaccination exposes you to germs that your body learns how to resist.

It was the kind of thought that hit me with a lot of force. There we were, sitting in a park and talking, and it felt as if everything had shifted just a little.

Hall said that when he gives talks about his books, he makes this point, and he gets people to think back to their school days. Often, he reminds them, the biggest, most popular kids from high school didn't go on to do all that much in the world, almost as if they had nothing to prove. The kids who dealt with troubles tended to try "to make more of ourselves," he says. The oyster needs the irritation of the grain of sand, after all, to make a pearl.

What does "normal" get you, anyway? Dov Fox, a former lecturer at the University of Oxford, wrote an essay about the quest to conform and become normal that made a beautiful point. He referred to the classic French play *Cyrano de Bergerac*, which is about a brilliant swordfighter and poet who has no confidence in love because his nose is huge. Struggling to overcome this abnormality might have been part of what made him strive to be great, Fox wrote. "Perhaps Cyrano would have been happier simply to have been 'normal.'" Today, he might even have gotten a nose job and had a nice, calm life in the suburbs. "But we would have lost a greatness and sensitivity of soul . . . [which] would have lessened all of us."

I asked this question before, and it's a good time to ask it again: Who wants to be *average*?

Empire State Human

You have probably picked up by now that I'm not a big fan of growth hormone treatments. You might even think that my problem with the drugs is that I missed out on getting any and I'm just jealous. As theories go, it wouldn't be a bad one. But it's wrong. You see, I had my chance—and turned it down.

When I was about ten, doctors told my parents that hormones could increase my height, and suggested that maybe we should give this new treatment a try. The way I remember it, my parents were a little worried about the side effects, but they let me have a say in the decision. I remember being very scared of needles back then, and still can feel the tightness in my chest as we talked about the treatment. I was really worried about becoming a human pincushion. I told my folks I didn't want to do it, and that was that.

It was a lucky decision. These were the days before bioengineered hormones, when the stuff came from the glands of dead people who had willed their bodies to science. That's creepy enough, but researchers later discovered that the hormones carried a risk of a fatal brain disorder that killed people in England and France. Even though no Americans were affected, I was glad to discover that I hadn't been exposed to that risk.

Recently, I called my mom to ask about it. She sent me my X-ray from 1962, when I was five. The doctor's notes said that my hand size was roughly average for a three-year-old, but only in the tenth percentile for a kid of my age at the time. But she didn't need an X-ray to know how teeny I was.

My mother also told me that, way back then, growth hormone was suggested by a cousin of ours, Milton Jacobs, who is an endocrinologist. "He said that you were small and I ought to do something about it," she recalled.

So I called Milton, who is not just a cousin but a close friend, and about twenty-five years older

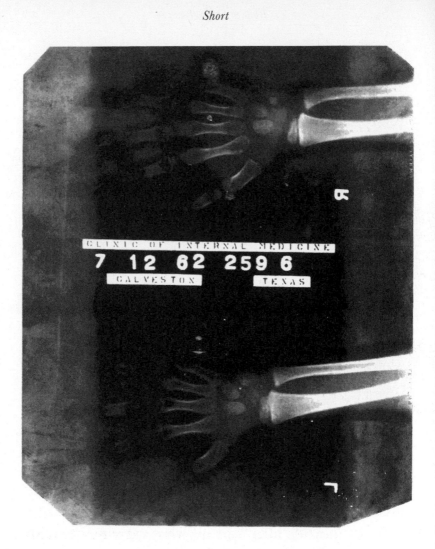

than I am. My wife and I chose the name Milton as the middle name for our youngest kid, so you know how I feel about him.

He seemed a little surprised to have the subject come up again after all these years. "I felt that it was worth the effort" to suggest the treatment, he said. He is tall himself, but felt that he had seen plenty of discrimination against shorter people. "I cared about you a great deal, and I still do," he said. "I didn't want you to carry any additional burden if you didn't have to." And so, he said, he had a conversation with my mother about the drugs.

As it turned out, he said, "you don't need to be tall [because] you can live with yourself very comfortably." And so, with the warmth of family love and hindsight, he told me, "I wouldn't have you change one fiber of your soul."

My mom said to me that later she heard about the medical problems with the old hormones and wanted to pat herself on the back. Once I said I didn't want to get the shots, she never looked back.

She told me, "I thought you were perfect."

So, as Milton says, I live with myself very comfortably. And yet, I occasionally feel a little flash of anger and can't tell what might set it off.

One day my family and I were hanging out with another family at the zoo. The other dad was a guy named Steve. He's nice, and has a kind of tough New York attitude that's a kick. He also towers over me, and is beefy, so the difference in our sizes when we walk together is pretty funny.

We were walking and talking, and the subject

of height came up. I told him that sometimes it seems like short guys don't get taken seriously.

He snorted. "You seem to be doing all right," he said. "Working at the *New York Times*."

"Steve, you don't understand," I shot back. "If I were six feet tall, I'd be president."

It was a pretty good joke, I thought, but he looked at me oddly, and I realized that I had also accidentally kind of insulted him. Because, you know, he's six feet tall. And he's not the president.

I'm not tall, but I've got a big mouth.

That conversation, by the way, happened before I had done all of this research into the studies. So I was walking around with a lot of misinformation in my head, and it weighed a little heavily on me: I had the feeling that the deck was stacked against me. And it left me with that little bit of heat, and that little bit of anger came out at the zoo.

I'm not the only one with a little bit of heat. Sitting in the cafeteria of my office not long ago, I was talking about my work on this book with a buddy of mine from work, Bill. He's only a little taller than I am, but it was the first time the subject of being short had ever come up between us. He too complained that studies showed how smaller guys are less likely to get the big jobs. I tried to explain what I had learned—that the studies don't say what they seem to say, and that even if they were right about general trends, it wouldn't necessarily have anything to do with him as an individual.

But as we talked, I could sense it. The little bit of heat was there. There was anger in his eyes, talking about prejudice against small guys.

Now, I'm talking about a very successful person here. He's working at this great newspaper and covering the entertainment industry, which makes him a pretty big guy in that world. The money he gets paid for writing books is more than I get paid in a year at my job. So what's his complaint?

Maybe, like most journalists, he's a complainer by nature. Or maybe it's a little resentment that comes from a feeling that whatever he may have achieved, he got it by having to work a little harder than the taller dudes who seem to have it so easy. It's an uncomfortable thought, but one that comes naturally to us all. It reminds me of what one of my favorite politicians, Ann Richards, used to say about women who achieve great things despite the prejudice against them. She had been governor of Texas, and had a great big cloud of white hair and a strong accent, and she told the people at the Democratic National Convention, "If you give us a chance, we can perform." She brought up one of the great ballroom dancing couples from the movies.

"After all," she said, "Ginger Rogers did

everything that Fred Astaire did. She just did it backwards and in high heels."

You don't have to be a woman to get that joke, or to feel the little bit of heat behind it.

But maybe, deep inside, like me, my friend Bill thinks he'd have done *even better* if he'd been taller. Remember the focusing illusion? It's that inner voice that blames one thing—in the case of short people, our height—for anything we wanted but didn't get. So people like me could go through life feeling like somebody put the real goodies on a high shelf and the world didn't give us stepladders.

The focusing illusion, then, can be a big problem. And little guys can end up with a chip on our shoulder. But it doesn't have to be that way. And that's what the next chapter is all about.

The Taming Power
of the Small

The other day I was eating lunch at the office. I was sitting with a guy who writes about classical music, another who writes about physics and astronomy, and a guy, George, who is one of the top lawyers for the newspaper. We eat together fairly often, and enjoy each other's company. That day, we were talking about flying. I mentioned that I always ask for an exit-row seat.

George smiled with delight. "For the leg room?" he asked.

Zing! He knew that I don't require a lot of space

to stretch my legs. But I do need room to open my laptop and work comfortably. But he couldn't help taking a shot at me.

The jokes never really go away. I had no quick comeback for George, but I don't need one anymore. Like my tall friend Gregg, I'm happy with the way things have turned out.

That's why I think Stephen Hall is right. Growing up short meant that I learned to take a lot of ribbing and an occasional pounding. But it also taught me to be funny and to be fast—both useful traits. It seems a lot of my childhood and teen years were spent building up Olivardia's "anchors."

Let's get back to my Grandma Clara for a moment. She gave me more than raccoon eyes and shrimpiness. I also inherited her tendency to be a little more likely to form blood clots than most other people. These can lead to strokes, heart attacks, and other medical problems. (Thanks again, Grandma!) I found out that I had the blood clot thing because of an eye problem I had a few years ago.

I lost some of the vision in my right eye. It turned out I had a tiny clot in the blood vessels at the back of my eye that messed up my vision. It was scary, but eventually I got better. I took some genetic tests that proved that I had a messed-up gene. And I knew that I'd inherited that gene from Clara, who suffered so much because of her stroke sixteen years before she died. I think my father's got the same genetic problem that Clara and I do, and sure enough, he's had two strokes. But he bounced back from each one—partly because medical science is better today, but also because he takes better care of himself than his mother did. His body was better prepared for trouble than hers was. Mine is, too, because I try to eat right and get regular exercise.

Just as I have tried to toughen up my body against the medical problems that might pop up down the road, I spent a lot of my childhood and teen years toughening up my personality so that it could take the hits. I'm not saying I did this intentionally; it just happened, pretty much. But it did make a difference.

In school, I built up human capital like crazy. I did a little of everything—except for sports. I might have made a decent wrestler, but in my town in Texas, when I was a kid, wrestling was not a sport. There was football, of course, and other sports like basketball and swimming, but I wasn't just small, I was slow, weak, and wimpy. The coaches were far more interested in the big, strong guys they had around them than little Johnny Schwartz.

That left plenty of other things to get involved with. My clarinet playing was good enough to get me into the school orchestra by high school, though not first chair; I put up with marching band, which went with it. I had fun in student government, becoming a vice president of the student council. I helped start a school newspaper and ran the school store. I was one of two white members of the Black History Club, and even acted in a play (badly). I was an announcer on the school radio program and picked up weekend work at the local radio station in town, where I got to geek out, in those days before personal computers, on the station controls. The other radio geeks and I learned how to produce sound effects on the ancient reel-to-reel tape machines and how to edit audiotape with an X-Acto knife.

I got to know the other people who worked at the station, including Hank Henderson, the announcer with the beautiful voice and only one arm, whose hand flew over the switches and knobs. He'd joke, "I can work anything in the station 'cept for the flit gun" (the pump-action bug spray gun, which required two hands). Nothing seemed to slow *him* down; why would I ever be worried about *height*?

All of those activities helped me to make friends, to fit in, and to show me that I was pretty good at a lot of things—good at, most of all, writing. When I won medals at the University Interscholastic League journalism competitions and went to state in editorial writing—a category my teacher entered me into on a whim—I got an inkling that this writing thing might end up being good for me.

I still carry the medal in my backpack. It says "Journalism."

Anne Case, the Princeton researcher, told me that she has doubts about the human capital argument. By her calculation, once you put intelligence into the mix and take out all the kids who are small because of developmental delays that drag the group's mental scores down, you don't really need the clubs and sports to have the same advantages as the tall guys.

That may be true. I'm no economist. I'm not even very good at math. But I wouldn't have given up anything that I did in school; it was too much fun.

True, there's no getting around the fact that some women just won't date shorter guys. Many sperm banks don't even take donations from smaller guys because too many women shopping for parental genes seem to find height important.

Take a quick look at the online personal ads and you'll find women who don't want to even consider dating smaller guys. On Craigslist, a "6' tall redhead" in San Francisco writes, "Guys shorter than 5'10", please click the BACK button now." Then there's this charmer in New York: "I like tall men because I am tall, so please no short men. If you're not sure if you're tall then it means that you are short, clearly."

Some of these women want it all: "Please be my height (5'10") or taller. Please also be a genius or at least an Ivy League grad." Don't forget rich and powerful, honey! Good luck with that!

Yes, they are out there. A lot of other women, though, proclaim right out that they don't care how tall a man is. A woman in New York looking for a guy said she doesn't want an overweight guy, but writes, "I couldn't care less, by the way, how tall or short you are."

So where does that leave short guys like me? Some women, clearly, see height as a deal breaker. But it's certainly not every woman, and many of the ones who say they want a tall guy are willing to reconsider if they meet the right man—like the woman in New York who wrote, "Like tall, dark, and handsome, but someone with a good heart and family oriented comes in many packages; I am willing to open all kinds. :)"

A short guy won't have much of a chance with some women—just as a guy who isn't rich won't have much of a chance with some women, and guys who aren't radiantly handsome with a cleft chin and curly hair won't have much of a chance with some women.

That leaves a lot of women in the world. And why would you want to hook up with such superficial snobs anyway?

One day I was walking down a Manhattan sidewalk with Bill Barol, one of the funniest guys I know. He's neither short nor tall, but he pointed to a stunningly good-looking, tall couple walking by us on the sidewalk. "You know, John," he said, "girls who look like that are always with guys who look like that." He's a comedy writer today, and he's happily married to a beautiful woman who is a television producer.

Just for fun, type "I love him because he makes me laugh" into Google. The last time I did it, I got nearly four thousand matches. Now type in "I love him because he's tall." Here's what I got:

> ***Your search—"i love him because he's tall"—did not match any documents.***

Most of all, I think the main reason I might have done all right with girls since high school could be that I carried myself in a way that said I didn't *feel* like a short, desperate guy. Because the biggest turnoff for women isn't shortness. It's the loser vibe. So I've found that walking with a little confidence—looking people in the eye instead of looking at my shoes, and giving people a smile—does a lot of good.

Height has never blocked me in my career, either. Nobody ever asked for it on my employment applications. Some of the people with whom I've had job interviews have even been shorter than I am.

Height simply has never come up. How tall do you have to be to be a reporter, anyway? My fingers reach the keyboard.

If there has ever been anything in my way, it wasn't height but status. I was trying to break in to a world that's top-heavy with graduates of the best universities—sophisticated Ivy Leaguers. A lot of 'em, I would later discover, were also pretty well off financially. That wasn't me. I was a state-school boy without a ton of money. But that didn't stop me, either.

About twenty years ago, I was getting ready to interview for my first job in big-time journalism: a writing gig at *Newsweek* magazine. I had the new suit and the uncomfortable shoes, and a pretty good stack of published stories to hand around. The night before getting on the plane—for fun, or out of nervousness, or simply because I know how—I pulled out my copy of the *I Ching*.

I don't even remember now how I ended up reading the *I Ching*, which is an ancient Chinese text that some people use in the West for fortune-telling. You use coins or straws to create a set of lines called a hexagram. That leads you to a passage of text that supposedly applies to your question. I've never been big on superstition, so I guess that shows how intimidated I was about the job interview. I formed a question in my head: Should I act like some kind of hotshot, or just be myself?

The hexagram that emerged from the ritual of flipping coins was one I had not seen before:

The passage that it led to was called "The Taming Power of the Small," and it said:

The Taming Power of the Small
Has success.
Dense clouds, no rain from our western region.

What did it mean? I still have no idea, honestly. I don't believe in fortune-telling. But reading the passage gave me a kind of reassurance: It's okay to be small. It's okay, in fact, to *go in* small, to not make a huge deal of myself, to be just me. That's the interpretation I came up with, anyway.

I got the job.

Over the years, I have even found my lack of height is useful. I sometimes make jokes about being little to make people laugh, which is disarming and puts them in a good mood to talk with me. And now and then, a short joke has really saved me.

Here's my best example: Early in my reporting days, I went down to Delaware to cover a lawsuit. It was a big deal at the time—something to do with a huge corporate merger—and the courthouse was packed with reporters. I got there early and sat through the morning part of the trial, and then the judge announced a lunch break. When I got back, though, the swarm of reporters around the door had gotten even bigger, and a gruff old guard was announcing that there was no more room for people to get in. I really needed to be in there—otherwise, the trip was wasted and I would have a hard time writing a story about the trial without the inside-the-courtroom stuff. Other reporters felt the same way, and they were complaining and shouting. The guard started closing the door, but I caught his eye and said, "Look—I'm *really small*, and I won't take up any room at all." Then an amazing thing happened. He smiled. And he reached over the shoulders of the two or three people between me and him, grabbed me by the shoulder of my jacket, and pulled me through the crowd and into the room.

A few years ago I met Morton Mintz, a pioneer of investigative journalism and a hero of mine. We knew each other by e-mail but hadn't come face-to-face until that night. "John!" he said. "I had a completely different mental image of you!" Then he stopped, too polite to say more.

"I know," I said. "I write taller."

The Beginning

So here we are, at the end of the book and the beginning of everything else. This is the part where I'm supposed to tell you some inspirational stuff and send you out to conquer the world. That's what final chapters tend to do, and who am I to argue with history?

Besides, you *can* conquer the world, or at least your part of it.

If I've done what I set out to do, you are now armed for battle—intellectual battle anyway. You know that you can be exceptional, whatever might be going on with the averages. Averages aren't destiny, and you're anything but average. You have picked up some strategies for coming out ahead and for seeing yourself as somebody who can win—not somebody who is born to lose. You're ready to go on and have anything but a second-rate life.

You can, I hope, be satisfied with who you are. No, wait. Not just satisfied. Happy.

Read books that make you laugh. (I love Terry Pratchett, the British novelist who makes me laugh out loud and makes me think.) Load your iPod with music that makes you smile. I've crammed mine full of great songs about being short, like Human League's wonderfully catchy "Empire State Human" and Ben Folds Five's "One Angry Dwarf." You can find those online, but I don't expect you to like what I like; I'm an old guy. You'll build your own playlist. You'll find your own songs.

Wait. Don't just be happy. Be proud.

There's a scene I love in the movie *The Commitments* when the character named Jimmy Rabbit tells the band of Irish misfits that they can make something of themselves if they try. He suggests that they take their inspiration from the civil rights movement in the United States. Even though times were hard and there was discrimination against black people, he explained, the activists chanted, "Say it loud—I'm black and I'm proud."

So yes, be proud.

And not just proud either. There's something even more important: Be yourself.

I know, who else would you be? But it's not as obvious as it sounds, and another movie helps explain why.

Rent the very cool film *Waking Life*, and watch the scene with a guy in a classroom talking about philosophy and, yes, the meaning of life. The guy is Robert Solomon, a real professor of philosophy at the University of Texas.

Bob died a few years ago. He was a good friend of mine, and I miss him every day. I've thought a lot about the things that he taught me, which are summed up pretty neatly by his comment in the film: "It's always *our* decision who we are."

Bob, by the way, was pretty darned short. And he was born with a weak heart and lived with a sense that life was a fragile thing. In other words, some people would say that he had been dealt a bad hand and might not have expected much from life. Bob would have disagreed though—I never met a happier, funnier guy. I never met anyone who was more deeply engaged in the art of living and living well.

Bob existed in a no-whining zone and taught

thousands of students that life is not what's handed to you, but what you make of it through your choices. Like he said in the movie, "It's always *our* decision who we are."

He walked tall.

You will, too.

Source Notes

This book was drawn from many sources—scientific papers; magazine articles; websites; comic books; interviews with researchers and people whose work gives them something to say about height, shortness, and just plain being different.

As a newspaper reporter, I learn things by reading and by talking with people. Interviews with some of the people quoted in this book shaped it and my thinking, and they have my gratitude. Some of those interviewed include the following:

Dan Barry, author, *Pull Me Up: A Memoir*; Bob Boniface, General Motors; Consuelo Bova, www.forthefit.com; Anne Case, Princeton University; Alice Dreger, bioethicist; Gordy Celestine, childhood friend; Dov Fox, former lecturer in political theory at the University of Oxford; Stephen S. Hall, science journalist; Milton Jacobs, cousin and endocrinologist; Gregg Lambdin, childhood friend; Roberto Olivardia, Harvard Medical School; Andrew Postlewaite, University of Pennsylvania; Alan D. Rogol, University of Virginia Health System; Judith Ross, Thomas Jefferson University; David E. Sandberg, University of Michigan Medical School; Marilyn Schwartz, my mom (Hi, Mom!)

Scientific Papers and Articles

Throughout the text, I refer to specific psychology and sociology studies. But I had to read many more to get a solid sense of the realities of height research. Not everyone is going to dive in and read a lot of heavy-duty research from scientific journals, but it's good to know what's out there. Where possible, I've listed hypertext links that take you directly to the paper; in other cases it takes you to a site that allows you to purchase the article. Many school libraries have subscriptions to online research services that will let you get the papers for free.

If you do dive into reading research, remember to keep an eye out for possible sources of bias.

Articles cited in the text:

The Fixers

"Growth Hormone Treatment for Short Stature: Inferences from FDA Decisions and Clinical Practice." *Atrium: The Report of the Northwestern Medical Humanities and Bioethics Program* 3 (2006): 13–15.
(bioethics.northwestern.edu/atrium/pdf/atriumissue3.pdf)

Sandberg, David E., William M. Bukowski, Caroline M. Fung, and Robert B. Noll. "Height and Social Adjustment: Are Extremes a Cause for Concern and Action?" *Pediatrics* 114 (2004): 744–50.
(pediatrics.aappublications.org/cgi/reprint/114/3/744.pdf)

Sandberg, David E., and Melissa Colsman. "Growth Hormone Treatment of Short Stature: Status of the Quality of Life Rationale." *Horm Res* 63 (2005): 275–83.
(content.karger.com/ProdukteDB/produkte.asp?Aktion=ShowFulltext&ArtikelNr=000086593&Ausgabe=231131&ProdukteNr=224036)

Does Size Matter?
CAESAR 3-D Anthropometric Database (brochure)
(store.sae.org/caesar/caesarbrochure.pdf)

Why Ross Perot Will Never Be President
Persico, Nicola, and Andrew Postlewaite. "The Effect of Adolescent Experience on Labor Market Outcomes: The Case of Height." *Journal of Political Economy* 112, no. 5 (2004): 1019–53.
(www.econ.upenn.edu/~apostlew/paper/pdf/short.pdf)

Doom and Gloom
Case, Anne, and Christina Paxson. "Stature and Status: Height, Ability, and Labor Market Outcomes." NBER Working Paper No. 12466. Center for Health and Wellbeing, Princeton University, August 2006.
(www.nber.org/papers/w12466)

Persico, Nicola, and Andrew Postlewaite. "The Effect of Adolescent Experience on Labor Market Outcomes: The Case of Height." *Journal of Political Economy* 112, no. 5 (2004): 1019–53.

Sandberg, David E., William M. Bukowski, Caroline M. Fung, and Robert B. Noll. "Height and Social Adjustment: Are Extremes a Cause for Concern and Action?" *Pediatrics* 114 (2004): 744–50.
(pediatrics.aappublications.org/cgi/reprint/114/3/744.pdf)

Sandberg, David E., and Melissa Colsman. "Growth Hormone Treatment of Short Stature: Status of the Quality of Life Rationale." *Horm Res* 63 (2005): 275–83. (content.karger.com/ProdukteDB/produkte.asp?Aktion=ShowFulltext&ArtikelNr=000086593&Ausgabe=231131&ProdukteNr=224036)

Bullies

Fox, Dov. "Human Growth Hormone and the Measure of Man." *New Atlantis*, no. 7 (Fall 2004/Winter 2005): 75–87. (www.thenewatlantis.com/publications/human-growth-hormone-and-the-measure-of-man)

Sandberg, David E., William M. Bukowski, Caroline M. Fung, and Robert B. Noll. "Height and Social Adjustment: Are Extremes a Cause for Concern and Action?" *Pediatrics* 114 (2004): 744–50. (pediatrics.aappublications.org/cgi/reprint/114/3/744.pdf)

Sandberg, David E., and Melissa Colsman. "Growth Hormone Treatment of Short Stature: Status of the Quality of Life Rationale." *Horm Res* 63 (2005): 275–83. (content.karger.com/ProdukteDB/produkte.asp?Aktion=ShowFulltext&ArtikelNr=000086593&Ausgabe=231131&ProdukteNr=224036)

Articles for further reading:

Cohane, Geoffrey H., and Harrison G. Pope, Jr. "Body Image in Boys: A Review of the Literature." *International Journal of Eating Disorders* 29, no. 4 (2001): 373–39.
(This study cites research that states that 67 percent of boys want to be taller.)
(www.ncbi.nlm.nih.gov/pubmed/11285574)

Hall, Stephen S. "The Short of It." *New York Times*, October 16, 2005.
(www.nytimes.com/2005/10/16/magazine/16growth.html)

Hall, Stephen S. "With His Bells and Curves, Human Growth Science Grew Up." *New York Times*, March 1, 2005.
(www.nytimes.com/2005/03/01/science/01tann.html)

Lee, Mary M., M.D. "Idiopathic Short Stature." *New England Journal of Medicine* 354 (June 15, 2006): 24.
(content.nejm.org/cgi/content/short/354/24/2576)

New York Times Health Guide to Growth Hormone
(health.nytimes.com/health/guides/test/growth-hormone/news-and-features.html)

New York Times Health Guide to Short Stature
(health.nytimes.com/health/guides/symptoms/short-stature/overview.html)

Ross, Judith L., David E. Sandberg, Susan R. Rose, Ellen Werber Leschek, Jeffrey Baron, John J. Chipman, Fernando G. Cassorla, Charmian A. Quigley, Brenda J. Crowe, Kristen Roberts, and Gordon B. Cutler, Jr. "Psychological Adaptation in Children with Idiopathic Short Stature Treated with Growth Hormone or Placebo." *Journal of Clinical Endocrinology & Metabolism* 89, no. 10 (2004): 4873–78. (jcem.endojournals.org/cgi/content/full/89/10/4873)

Sandel, Michael J. "The Case Against Perfection." *The Atlantic*, April 2004, at 50.
(www.theatlantic.com/doc/200404/sandel)

Voss, Linda D. "Is Short Stature a Problem? The Psychological View." *European Journal of Endocrinology* 155 (2006): S39–S45. (www.eje-online.org/cgi/content/full/155/suppl_1/S39)

Further Reading and Viewing

Throughout the text, I've referred to Stephen S. Hall's book for adults *Size Matters: How Height Affects the Health, Happiness, and Success of Boys—and the Men They Become* (Boston: Houghton Mifflin Harcourt, 2006). In Chapter 6, I also quoted Dan Barry's book *Pull Me Up: A Memoir* (New York: W.W. Norton & Company, 2001). Anyone who likes this book and who would like to dig deeper into the meaning of the science and culture behind height consciousness should read them. (Like all of the books I'll refer to here, they can be tough going for younger readers.

But you never know what's too hard to read until you try.)

To focus on the ways that statistics are used, misused, and abused in daily life, there's a classic old book that everybody ought to read. *How to Lie with Statistics*, by Darrell Huff and illustrated by Irving Geis (New York: W. W. Norton, 1954), is just 144 pages. Some of the examples are really out of date, but the lessons are timeless. And it makes statistics funny!

A more recent book that looks at statistics in the world of science and health, and at how the news media doesn't always get it right, is *News and Numbers: A Guide to Reporting Statistical Claims and Controversies in Health and Other Fields* by Victor Cohn and Lewis Cope (Hoboken, NJ: Wiley-Blackwell, Second edition 2001). It's used in a lot of schools and colleges to teach students who want to be writers how to get it right.

To learn more about how a condition like being short gets turned into a semi-medical problem with a disease-ish name such as "growth failure problem," there's *The Medicalization of Society: On the Transformation of Human Conditions into Treatable Disorders* by Peter Conrad (Baltimore: Johns Hopkins University Press, 2007).

And although it's out of print, if you ever get a chance, read the children's book *The Boy Who Fooled the Giant* by Tamara Kitt (New York: Putnam Publishing Group, 2000; First edition 1963). It's a sweet story about how a small person can do big things.

For a laugh, rent the movie *Time Bandits*, directed by Terry Gilliam (Avco Embassy Pictures/Handmade Films, 1981). It's funny, and funny is always good. But it's worth watching the whole film, about a band of guys who travel through time to steal treasure, for a monologue by the actor playing a height-obsessed Napoleon Bonaparte, the famously small emperor of France, who gives a drunken speech on the accomplishments of other smallish leaders.

"Alexander the Great?" he asks. "Five feet, *exactly*. Isn't that incredible? . . . Oliver Cromwell? The only man with any guts in British history. Not a big man at all."

Oh, how I laughed. And you will, too.

Index

Baggins, Frodo, 45
Barol, Bill, 106
Barry, Dan, 70
Behavioral studies
    problems with, 52–53
Beijing Institute of
        External Fixation
        Technology, 6
Bell curve
    defined, 16–17
    relativity of, 18
Berra, Yogi, 40–41
Bilger, Burkhard, 34
Bloomberg, Michael,
        43, 59
Bodybuilders, 7
Bogues, Muggsy, 47
Boniface, Bob, 23
Bova, Consuelo, 24
*Boy Who Fooled the Giant,
        The* (Kitt), 42,
        122–23
Boys' departments, 25
Breasts
    sizes of, 9
Bullies, 66–72
Bullying, 49

C

CAESAR. *See* Civilian
        American and
        European Surface
        Anthropometry
        (CAESAR)
Case, Anne, 56–57,
        105
Causation
    versus correlation,
        54–55
Centers for Disease
        Control (CDC)
    chart published by,
        20
Children
    alliances formed by,
        82
    self image of, 13
    social issues, 13
China
    government
        discrimination in, 5
Civilian American and
        European Surface
        Anthropometry
        (CAESAR), 22–23

7/10